THE BABY MAMA CHRONICLES

By

Latisha Lenese Pitts, Sharon Denise Brown-Rivers & Tekeirra Tenese Brown

This book is dedicated to Baby Mamas everywhere.

The struggles of being a baby mama are real but you must laugh to keep from crying knowing that God is working all things out for your good!

"And we know that all things work together for good to them that love God, to them who are the called according to His purpose" (Romans 8:28).

Table of Contents

Preface... 4

1. Are You a Baby Mama?...5
2. Baby Mama's…The Good, The Bad & The Ugly……….9
3. The Married Baby Mama…………………………………..20
4. The Baby Daddy……………………………………………...28
5. The Good Baby Daddy……………………………………….40
6. Child Support, Oh Really!..47
7. Horror Stories……………………………………………….56
8. Testimonies…………………………………………………..82
9. Baby Mama 101: Things Every Baby Mama Should Know…………………………………………………………...99
10. How to Avoid becoming a Baby Mama………………..114
11. Meet The Real Baby Mamas……………………………...116

Preface

The Baby Mama Chronicles was written by baby mamas for baby mamas. The authors of this book have over three decades of experience combined being baby mamas. The Baby Mama Chronicles was birthed out of Latisha's experience with her own baby daddies. The Baby Mama Chronicles provides readers with insight on the plight of the baby mama. This book was written to inspire, support, motivate and encourage baby mamas all over the country to keep moving forward. The Baby Mama Chronicles is a mixture of fact, fiction and Biblical principles. This book shines a light on the struggles that being a baby mama brings. It provides baby mamas with hope knowing that although their situation started off wrong with the help of the Lord they can recover, rebuild and have a happy ending.

Chapter One

Are You a Baby Mama?

Are You a Baby Mama?

You picked up this book didn't you? No, I'm kidding... but that did get your attention, so you might as well read on right? Right... but, before we get started, let's make sure that you have a complete understanding of what a baby mama is. Oh Urban Dictionary, where art thou? "A term used to define an unmarried young woman (but can be a woman of any age) who has had a child."

You might be a baby mama if...

Number One: You are not married and you had unprotected sex! You slipped up or you maybe didn't but now you are pregnant or you already have a kid or kids. Newsflash, you are officially somebody's baby mama. You were so in love with him that you believed everything he told you, believed every promise he made, not realizing that those promises would soon be broken. You believed that he would never leave you standing on the sidelines being simply the mother of his kid. Some days you are stuck between a rock and a hard place trying to keep everything together while keeping a smile on your face. It's hard, but you're going to have to keep pushing forward. Yes, there are days where you just want to strangle your baby daddy (and yourself) but, by the grace of God, you move on and stay strong.

Number Two: You're getting one or more of the following: WIC, TANIF, FOOD STAMPS, MEDICAID, or CHIPS and that's still not enough to help you take care of your kids! "Oh please" right? WRONG! Many baby mama's struggle every month to stretch what little resources they do have to provide for their kids with little to no financial help from their baby daddy or daddies. It's hard out here and remember, "the struggle is real" People might think that you're exaggerating but you're honestly not...taking care of kids is not cheap or easy. It's a full time job that you and your budget have to be one hundred percent committed to. If this sounds anything like you, you might want to keep on reading this book, it could come in handy.

Number Three: 24 hours a day, 7 days a week, 47 weeks of the year, you are the primary caregiver for your child or children. Your children are always with you. In fact, when people see you without them, they are shocked and astonished. They ask you questions like "where are the kids, today?" It takes a miracle or a holiday to get a week, weekday or weekend for yourself. When your kids are not with you, you actually start to feel like a piece of you is missing, it's uncomfortable, and you don't like it. Personal time has become a thing of your past. Your baby daddy promises over and over again to spend time with the kids but he almost always fails to come through. Then when you confront him about not seeing his child in weeks, he blows up in your face like you are to blame. You watch your child wait for a parent who's never there or always too late. You dry every tear your child cries because daddy refuses to put his kids at the top of his priority list.

Number Four: You are known everywhere you go as either that's such and such's mom or that's such and such's baby mama. "Oh there goes (Insert name here)'s baby mama"… I know you hate that, I know you do. You probably wonder if they even know your real name. Your identity has been merged with you kids and your baby daddy.

Number Five: You've ever felt like snapping, cracking and popping on your baby daddy because he never understands your struggle and he doesn't provide enough help. You argue with your kid's daddy about child support, spending enough quality time with your kid and putting your child's needs first. He simply doesn't understand what you're trying to say to him. It's like something in his small mind doesn't click and you don't understand why. You're mentally and physically tired of his emotional detachment. You even wonder why he even has kids. You're tired of his lies, games, disappointments, mess and confusion. You're tired of him avoiding or mistreating your children. You want him to change and grow up but the only thing that is changing is the year. You try to warn other women to be careful who they have a baby by, so that they won't be stuck in the same situation as you, going in circles with a baby daddy who acts worse than your kids.

Number Six: You have to laugh to keep from crying when you don't understand why your baby daddy doesn't care for the kids like you do. Fact of the matter is, he never does and he never will. You watch the things he does for other children and people and wonder why he doesn't do for his own kids. You see him spend hours with his friends and with his business but with his own seed he can't spend ten minutes. He spends his money on vehicles, shoes, clothes, food and his bills are paid and yet he doesn't even consider how his child's financial needs are being met. He never offers his help. Your child's calls are forwarded to voicemail so much the child has stopped leaving messages or stopped calling. Over the years, you've realized for yourself that your baby daddy is sorry. He doesn't try to do better and he doesn't care. You know it's not fair but you given up the fight. You refuse to waste another moment wondering why. You realized long ago that you can't make him be a good daddy to y'all kids. So now you laugh instead of crying because you see that your baby daddy is consistently inconsistent.

Number Seven: Your baby daddy has a girlfriend or even a wife! She thinks you still want him but the reality is that you don't. You just want him to take care of his kid or kids but she stays in your face keeping up mess, drama and confusion trying to secure her place. Whether she likes it or not, you will always be around (for the rest of that child's life) but she just can't handle it. Her insecurities got her so sure that you want to be in her place but again that's not the reality. The reality is that you've moved on and she needs to move on from the fact that you already had him and don't want him back.

Number Eight: You've got baby Mama Drama and, you don't even have a BABY? Yes, this is possible and this question is for the baby mommas who aren't baby mommas but still chose to read this book. You're obviously with a guy who has a baby momma or baby mommas and their drama is spilling over to you. See, what you have to realize is that you are what we call "The Step-Baby Mama" but we'll get into that a little later.

Number Nine: You want to be his baby mama. You love your man; you want to secure your position. You think having a baby by him will keep him with you. You think having his baby will be your ticket out of your current situation. You want a baby because you want some one to love and you someone to care for. Your convinced that you and your man will be together forever and having his baby will be the icing on the cake. You're not his wife but you are his full time permanent live in girlfriend and that's not enough. "Why not have his baby? We love each other!" Well keep reading and you will discover why not to become his baby mama.

If you can identify with any of these categories, read on because you are a baby mamma!

Chapter Two

Baby Mama's...The Good, The Bad & The Ugly

Before we can help you and write from your perspective, we need to help you classify the type of baby mama that you truly are or have been at some point in your life. To be honest over your time being a baby mama you have changed and evolved into the baby mama you are today. Yes, people change but there are some similarities that are universal to us all. This chapter will focus on a few of those universal qualities. No baby mama is the same as the other; there are many different types. However, it is very important that since you do in fact identify yourself as a baby mama, you know what type of baby mama you are. Read on my dear, read on.

The Good Baby Mama

This baby mama is cool, calm, collect and tries her best to stay patient with her kids and her baby daddy. The good baby mama is one of a kind. She takes care of her business and always gets the job done. She sets goals and she does what it takes to reach them, with or without her baby daddy. Men with money and material things do not impress her because she depends on God to supply all of her needs. The good baby mama is a woman who makes the necessary sacrifices for her kids at all times whether she feels like it or not. She provides for her kids without a second thought and gives them the best of everything she has. The good baby mama loves others unconditionally. She is transparent about her mistakes and turns them into life lessons for her children. The good baby mama keeps things real and she doesn't keep up mess, drama or confusion. She does not use her children to manipulate her baby daddy or any one else. She maintains a healthy balance and she raises her children so that they are able to function effectively in this world. She equips her children with wisdom, knowledge and understanding about the disappointments and hurt that is in the world. Her kids know that they always have her in their corner to comfort, guide and motivate them. The good baby mama knows how to keep her children in line and teaches them how to respects her as well as their daddy. She knows how to admit her mistakes and is not afraid to apologize. Although the good baby mama is independent, she is totally dependent on the Lord. She understands that God alone supplies all of her needs. The good baby mama knows the importance of having a relationship with the Lord and so she shows her children how to have their own relationship with Him. The good baby mama is a praying woman who teaches her kids how to pray. The good baby mama raises her children to honor and obey their daddy regardless of what he does or does not do for them. She is consistent and she exhibits all of the qualities of a Proverbs 31 women. The good baby mama is resourceful. She is always an asset and never a liability. The good baby mama is the baby mama we all strive to be.

Ms. Overly Nice

Also Known As, "I just like to keep it pleasant, polite, and respectful". This is the baby mama who is NO ONES baby mama, she is a mother! You are pleasant to deal with, polite to your baby daddy, and also respectful to the people you encounter. Ms. Overly Nice always wants to make sure that her baby daddy is happy with what she is doing with the kids and with herself. You are always looking to please everyone. You always have a big grin on your face and try to make yourself come off as perfect. If your baby daddy needs something, you're always there for him but he isn't always there for you. Ms. Overly Nice doesn't get upset with her baby daddy; she gets upset with herself or her kids. If something in her life isn't going right with her baby daddy, her life is ruined. You feel like you have to do whatever it takes to make him happy again. But how can you make someone else happy when you're not truly happy with yourself? If you had to think about that question, you MIGHT be Ms. Overly Nice.

The Lazy Baby Mama

Also Known as, "Ms. No Ambition". She doesn't want to work, doesn't want to go to school and just doesn't want to do anything that is productive to help her family. You take full advantage of your kids and don't care about anyone who has something to say about the way you live. Your house is never clean and your excuse for that is because you work full time and you don't feel like doing it. There is always an excuse for why you can't do something for your kids, but you don't mind going out with your friends or hanging out at the club. The lazy baby mama expects more from her baby daddy than she expects from herself. She sits around and waits for her baby daddy to do things that should have already been done and she doesn't mind "leeching" off of him. I mean after all, that is what he's there for right? If you're lying in your bed right now, reading this and the kids want you to take them outside to play, but your excuse is "I'm on the Internet right now, don't you see me updating my status?" Then, this might be you.

The Talker

Better known as, "Ms. Opinionated". This is the baby mama that just talks way too much, and doesn't shut up. This is definitely one of the baby mama's that you want to avoid becoming. She tells all her friends about what is going on between her and the baby daddy and doesn't care what she let slip off of her tongue. Ms. Opinionated will always have something to say for every situation even if the situation has nothing to do with her. She always feels like she has to put her two cents in your business and won't care what you have to say about it. The talker usually finds herself in weird situations because she gives out to much information about her life. She talks about a lot of stuff that she can't back up and often doesn't even remember that she said it. She probably won't even classify herself as talking too much; she'll simply just say that she's "opinionated". Look out for this type of baby mama. If this fits you, you might want to hush, and hush QUICK!

The Trapper

This baby mama got pregnant on purpose just to keep her man. You may never admit what you did but you did it. The Trapper secretly stopped using her birth control, had sex knowing she was ovulating, seduced him while he was intoxicated, poked a hole in the condom or didn't even use protection just so she could get her man's DNA and go half on a baby. You enticed him with sex to get pregnant. The Trapper is serious and swift. Your seduction is poisonous and always on point. The Trapper traps her man for many different reasons: security, money, attention, affection, fame and even marriage. Your baby daddy was a hit target but you didn't realize that a baby can't keep a man. After the child is born, the trapper will use the kid to manipulate and run game on her baby daddy. If you are a trapper, remember the game you play will backfire on you one day.

Ms. Show Me The Money

This baby mama is going to provide for her kids by all means necessary and doesn't care what it takes. You need your money on time because you don't have time for your baby daddy paying late. You will cuss out your baby daddy out at the drop of a dime if he is doing anything that gets in the way of you taking care of your kids. Ms. Show Me The Money is not afraid to put her hands on her baby daddy either. You have to make sure that your kids don't want for anything and you make sure that they have it all, and more. Your kids stay dressed in name brand clothes from head to toe, a new pair of shoes every month and the latest technology. This baby mama is nothing to play with, and won't settle for anybody who isn't making money. If it doesn't make money, then it doesn't make cents. Feel me?

Ms., Good Ain't Never Good Enough

Better known as "Ms. Unacceptable" also know as Ms. G.A.N.G.E. Your baby daddy can never live up to your standards because he is simply not as good as you want him to be and in your eyes he never will be. Ms. G.A.N.G.E is very unappreciative and whatever her baby daddy does for her kids or gives her kids is never good enough. Your baby daddy could be paying fifty thousand dollars a month in child support but you'll want $100,000. Ms. Unacceptable wants it all and she believes her kids deserve it all. You have put your children on the highest pedestal and in your eyes nothing your baby daddy gives them will be good enough and nothing he does will make him a good daddy. You have absolutely no respect for your baby daddy. You know why? Because you've been playing the mama and daddy role for so long. Ms. G.A.N.G.E. makes her own money, she pays her own bills, has her house together and won't settle for anyone who isn't on the same level that she is. Ms. Unacceptable believes that you don't need a man to raise your kids and she is all for single independent successful moms. If this sounds like you, you could be Ms. Unacceptable a.k.a. Ms. G.A.N.G.E.

The CRAZY Baby Mama

Also Known as "Psycho Mama". All baby mama's can all be a little crazy at times, but this baby mama is just over the top. You will wait outside your baby daddy's house, stalk his Facebook page, stalk his girlfriend, call his friends and family to ask about him and threaten your baby daddy if he refuses to be with you. Psycho Mama won't let her baby daddy get away from her and she will ALWAYS be around and make his life a living hell. Her baby daddy can't peacefully move on from her because she simply won't allow that to happen, so he has to run! Once you had his baby, that's it, he is your property (at least, that's what you think). You call his phone, email him, text him, Instagram him, and more until you can get into contact with him. And if he pisses you off, you will not hesitate to lay your hands on him, and then call the police like he is in the wrong. Psycho Mama is nuts, but don't let her know that, because you could wake up with your hair shaved off. She will use her kids as a way for her baby daddy to come and see her.

The Trapper is your best friend. Ladies, if this sounds familiar its not to late to change and stop being this type of baby mama.

Social Media Mama

DEFINETLY known as "Ms. Tweet My life". This baby mama literally puts all her business on the Internet. You can't even log onto a social media site without seeing a dramatic update from her. She is the absolute worst, people from Africa know that her baby daddy didn't come and see his kids today. You are super dramatic and extra on Facebook and Twitter; you'll mention your baby daddy on either one three or four times a day and your won't hesitate to let the world know if he missed a child support payment. You are always writing unnecessary things on your baby daddy wall and liking posts from other girls. Social Media Mama will comment on your pictures and say "Oh, so you can take pictures but, can't come see your kids?" leaving her baby daddy dazed and confused, making him feel like less of a person. Social Media mama couldn't have any real friends because she's always updating her cyber friends about what's going on in her life with her baby daddy. If your cyber life revolves around your baby daddy this might be you and if you're this baby mama, that stinks because your business is all in the street. Update that! #nostatusupdate #keepitpersonal #timeforachange #getittogether #keepyourbusinessoutthestreets

Ms. "So what you pay me child support, you still can't see your kids!"

It is as simple as that. There is no better-known name for this baby mama because she is what she is. She doesn't care what her baby daddy does for his kids, what he buys for his kids, or what he pays her in child support; he still can't see the kids because he just can't. You don't have a valid reason;

you're just another name for a female dog (Ladies, you know what that means, and if you don't, look it up). This baby mama takes her child support and gets her nails and hair done, but doesn't do half as much for the kids. He can't see his kids until he gets back with you, your feelings are hurt and child support won't change that. You threaten him with child support if he doesn't come see the kids at your house with you there. You always have an excuse for why he can't spend time with the kids alone or take them with him. You refuse to let your baby daddy build his own relationship with his kids. Why you ask? The answer to that is simple, because you are selfish, and you want your baby daddy for your self. If he can't build a relationship with you, then he can't build a relationship with the kids. That's just how it is and how it always will be. If you're this type of baby mama, you might need to re-evaluate yourself and set yourself free.

Ms. Bitteritta

Also known as "Ms. Unpleasant". This baby Mama is so bitter that it starts to spill over onto the kids. She barely wants to deal with her baby daddy, she surely doesn't want to budge or make any arrangements with him. If her baby daddy sets a specific date with her, he better make sure that he stick with it because if he doesn't than he's screwed. Her kids are the same way, if you don't stick to your plans; they're done dealing with you period. No one wants to deal with Ms. Bitteritta because they know how she is. However, you have a reason for being bitter. You have been let down so much in the past because you put your faith in your baby daddy instead of in God, and your baby daddy has constantly failed you and your kids. This has happened so many times that it has made you a very emotionally drained, stressed, unstable and void woman. Ladies, you want to avoid becoming Ms. Bitteritta by all means, if you're not bitter already. Choose to not be bitter one more day!

The Want To Be Baby Mama

Also known as Ms. " I want to have your baby" This is the lady who will do anything possible to make sure that she is the one having his baby. You are not a baby mama yet but you want to be. She will trick you into getting her pregnant. This baby mama maybe deceitful and cannot be trusted. The want to be baby mama always pressures her man to go ahead and have kids with her. She's always trying to go look at the baby stuff whenever you go to the store with her. The want to be baby mama is very overbearing and is always talking about "The future" and having kids. You are obsessed with having a baby and you are always reminding your man when you are ovulating although he really doesn't care. This baby mama can be a handful and if this is you, you need to stop, drop and roll… right on to the crazy house.

The Repeat Offender

Last but DEFINETLY not least is the repeat offender. This baby mama doesn't have any aliases or anything because her name describes her good enough. This baby mama just doesn't learn and doesn't care too learn. She falls into the same cycle every time and part of the reason is because she falls into lust quickly thinking its love. That's exactly how she finds herself pregnant every time. The Repeat offender has different baby daddies and they all keep up a lot of drama. She didn't learn from the first time and may not learn from the third time. The Repeat offender isn't ashamed of being a baby mama to multiple men; she's only ashamed that they left her. Well, she isn't even ashamed of that, or she wouldn't be doing the same things over and over. The repeat offender has been all of the baby mama's listed above on her baby mama journey, at least one time. She has been Crazy, Lazy, Overly Nice, A Talker, Stays on social Media, A Trapper (I mean, She is trapping those guys right), A Dangler and Bitter. If this is you, please know that you are very fertile and kids are expensive.

Chapter Three

The Married Baby Mama

Well, you made it to chapter 3… (Whew) I bet you have learned even more than you already know about being a baby's mama? Ok! Here's a little more interesting information that could be very helpful to you now or in the future. This chapter of the book talks about the married baby mama. I guess you may be saying to yourself, you are not a baby mama. I beg to differ, because you probably have a baby, you're probably married or engaged and I am guessing you are a woman? If you answered yes to these questions, then I would say you are a married baby mama. Now, that we have this sorted out let me talk about the different types of married baby mamas and clarify each type in more detail.

The Baby Mama of a Limited or Absent Spouse

This is a married baby mama with a husband who is rarely home, maybe due to his career, or some other unforeseen reason. In either case, this baby mama is usually the one who takes care of the children's physical, emotional and medical needs on a daily basis with limited or no help from the daddy. This type of baby mama is usually with the children 24 hours a day, 7 days a week and often feels like she is raising the children on her own. Well, girl let me tell you something, you are! So, what you need to do is take care of your children to the best of your ability, make a little time for yourself and when your significant other returns home let him take over some. Let's face it girl, we have our hands full each day trying to maintain the married wife's role and the single baby mamma's role. Take the kids to school, pick them up, go to work, fix dinner, clean the house, do routine maintenance, be the nurse, home school for some, help spouse with his business needs or personal needs that he can't do while at work and the list goes on and on. We are usually exhausted from our roles as being a married/single baby mama and a lot of times the husbands don't understand.

The Baby Mama with the Cheating Spouse with His No Good Self

This is a woman with a husband who cheats and obtains a baby outside of his marriage. Now, you have to deal with a baby mamma yourself and I'm sure you have a lot to say about that. This type of married baby mama is usually resentful, deeply disappointed with her spouse, may not trust her spouse any longer and may have contemplated a divorce at one time or another. What you really need to do is first come to grip with the fact that your husband got a child outside of your marriage. You need to ask yourself is this marriage worth saving and if you are willing to forgive your husband truly for his mistake? If you are willing to do these things, then you must ask yourself if you are willing to treat this other child with love and respect. Meaning, don't treat the child in a negative or abusive manner because you are pissed at your spouse or at the other baby mama. Also, you must be willing to have a mature and respectful relationship with the other baby mamma when it comes to things that are related to the other child. Another thing, make sure that you treat the other child in the same exact manner as you treat your child or children, if you have any, because this child can't help the fact that your husband obtained him/her outside of marriage. A lot of times I see people who I know that fall into this category try to compete with the baby mama and I'm like why? For one thing, don't you still have your husband? Is he still taking care of your household, in other words bring you home the cash? Is he being the attentive man you once married, the loving father to your kids, respectful, honest and the love of your life? If you answered yes to all of these questions then you don't have anything to compete with. Ok! Just take care of your family, put your faith into the hands of the Lord and do what's right.

The Extra Baggage Married Baby Mama

She has children that she came into the marriage with. This type of baby mama can come with a lot of drama if she's not handling her business right and if this is you, listen up. First of all, do you want your husband or your baby daddy? Because if it's your baby daddy, honey child you better handle that for sure. Now, if you truly want your husband then you need to respect the word husband. I know most of you believe that your children come first and they do in certain situations, but in a marriage God is first, your husband is second, the children are next and so on. So, what I am saying is that when you have a God fearing, faithful spouse and you have a child or children outside of your marriage you need to involve your spouse totally. You all need to get together to discuss how you are going to handle the situation, when it comes to visitation, child support and etc. This is because it is better when everyone is involved in the process, so things won't get out of hand or be misunderstood by either party, which could create unneeded conflict. Also, since majority of the time the husband is taking care of the spouse other child, he will probably feel that he has a right to be involved in the entire situation. This will provide your husband with more confidence in the marriage as well, because he won't feel threatened. Some children actually love the idea of having the step dad and biological dad so create and maintain a situation where your husband and baby daddy can be respectful to one another. Now, I didn't say they have to be buddies, just respectful and cordial to one another. Finally, stick to what you say when it comes to your baby daddy and don't be flirting with him on the side or hooking up with him on the down low. You are too precious and beautiful for that anyway and your relationship with your husband is too valuable to let your baby daddy come in between it. Don't forget some baby daddy's try to throw shade up at the spouse; I am telling you for your own good don't stand for this because if he was all that he would be in the shoes that your husband are wearing. So take care of your business Mrs. Wifey/Baby Mama!

The Step Baby Mama

This is the wife that secretly wants to be the real baby mama and may be jealous at times. Then again, she may be happy that she isn't the real mama, because some kids are a hot mess, but that is another book. The step mama may try to take on the mother's role when the children are over, she may be overly helpful, or maybe not helpful at all. The first thing you need to remember is that you are the stepparent so don't try to take over the mother's role. Be that supportive wife and love your stepchildren as your own and try to maintain a trustworthy and respectful relationship with that child. Don't be questioning the child about his/her mother or your husband and don't try to compete with the other parent. If for some reason, your stepchild is not willing to have a relationship with you, this is something you and your husband need to discuss. Then as a family all of you all can sit down as a family to determine why and to possibly seek a positive solution to the problem. If that doesn't help the relationship, you may need to seek assistance from a family counselor.

Mrs. Got to Have Everything Perfect

This baby mama tries to make sure the house stays tidy, the meals are cooked, the children are all so perfect, the husband is taken care of and everything is just great all the time. If this type of baby mama is you, let me be the first to tell you to lighten up. Because in the end you're going to wear your brain cells out and create more problems for yourself. For one thing, you are going to make your kids and spouse get accustomed to you trying to make everything so perfect, then when you get burnt out and stop they will be disappointed. This eventually will create possible arguments, resentment and other problems. Also, your spouse and children will expect you to cater to all of their needs and somewhat take advantage of you. They won't be willing to do anything because they know you will do it for them. Such as cooking all the time, taking care of the children non-stop, cleaning on your own with no or very limited help from them and so on. Mrs. Lady, everything doesn't have to be perfect all the time, live some and have some fun. As long as the house stays decent, the kid's needs are taking care of, your relationship is good and you are happy, that is what it is all about. Having everything so perfect all the time will make you crazy. I can honestly tell you that, because I was once this type of baby mama and I use to run myself crazy and run my family loco. So loosen up, relax and have fun with your family and live your life, because days go by fast and before you know it, it's all over.

The Try to be Slick Baby Mama

This baby mama takes care of children and household in general, however, she may use her children to help her scheme additional things out of her spouse. She may or may not have a man on the side but if she does, she may use her children as an alibi. In other words, tell her husband she's taking the children somewhere, when in fact she's out meeting another man or hanging out with undesirable friends. This lady tries to be very clever, schooling her children to what to say or not say and carefully planning all of her trickery. If this is you, I 'm not here to judge or tell you what you should or shouldn't do because you are a grown woman. The only question that I need for you to address to yourself is regarding your inner happiness. Are you truly satisfied with yourself and your relationship? See a lot of times women who tend to play around and involve their children in personal fiascos like this are really unhappy with their relationship and want more. I know this first hand because I have personal experience with this type of married baby mama. This type of person really can't be trusted and often is a straight up user. She often accuses her spouse of cheating because she's cheating, she may engage in recreational drugs or alcohol and likes to hang out in clubs and other places. This type of married baby mama will never have the real relationship that she tries to pretend to have and eventually the children will slip up and tell or get mad and tell if they know. Remember, what is often done in the dark, will eventually come to light and when it does it's going to take a lot to make everything right. Furthermore, you need to realize some children will cover for their parents for as long as they can and a lot won't. However, regardless most children will still be resentful toward their parent for having a relationship outside of their marriage. So trust, don't be a Slick Married Baby Mama, be a trusting married baby mama.

The Married Baby Mama We All Strive to Be

These types of married baby mama usually have everything all together, mentally, physically, emotionally, spiritually, financially and all. Granted, it takes most of us a long time to be this type of married baby mama. But we can do it with a prayer, help, determination, intelligence, dedication and motivation. First we have to understand the type of married baby mama we are and want to be and if that baby mama isn't the one you want to be it's up to you to make a change. We need to instill in our spouses the things that we expect him to do in regards to being a supportive spouse and daddy. We need to let go of any insecurities that could prevent us from accomplishing our family and personal goals. We must learn and find out new or added ways to be a productive, happy and loving wife and mother. We need to focus on the things that make us satisfied as women, spouses and mothers, because once that is accomplished, the possibilities are limitless. Most of all we need to instill prayer into our daily lifestyles, because things don't blossom as they should without prayer. Then we all need to be determined to be the married baby mama we all strive to be and work like heck to be good at it. Personally, I am stressing to you it is hard being a married baby mama and things do get difficult but in the end it will be all worth it. Just keep your trust in God, be who HE designed you to be, take care of your children and remember we are in this together. From one married baby mama to the next married baby mama, embrace your title and tell the haters to step aside. Now, on to the next chapter.

Chapter Four

The Baby Daddy

The Bad Baby Daddy

The bad baby daddy can be characterized as a man who fails to take on the responsibility of being a good dad to his child or children. All children need support spiritually, emotionally, physically, financially, socially & academically. The bad baby daddy fails to meet one or more of the basic needs of his children. In some instances, the bad baby daddy sees nothing wrong with leaving his child's basic needs unmet & this is a serious problem. Often times the bad baby daddy will place his social life, his wants and his desires before the basic needs of his child which leaves the mother to handle all of the responsibility of raising the child. It appears as if the bad baby daddy could careless about the child that he helped bring into this world. Thus, leaving the child's mother to deal with frustration, bitterness, anger and regret. Ladies, the bad baby daddy is to be avoided at all cost. He is a vehicle for confusion, disorder, unhappiness, disappointment, anger and sorrow. The bad baby daddy may never learn from his mistakes. Oftentimes, the bad baby daddy takes his character flaws to his grave, never providing adequate support to his children. The only way to help the bad baby daddy is to pray for him. Only Jesus can create the change that woman and children need to see in these types of men.

Beware the bad baby daddy is in a city near you!

Mr. Let's Go Half On A Baby
(a.k.a. Mr. LGHOB)

Ladies always remember to run and run fast from Mr. Let's Go Half On A Baby! This is the guy that wants you to have his kid but doesn't want the commitment. He believes that loving you is giving you his seed. This guy is not interested in making you his wife; he just wants to ruin your life. He wants to give you the baby mama status as a tool to control you and limit you. Mr. LGHOB wants you to have his kid. Everything is all good during the baby making process but after the baby is born, reality sets in. Mr. LGHOB is nothing to play with. He makes all of these promises before the baby is born and then once the child is delivered, he does absolutely nothing. He is a super disappointment who leaves baby mama's full of regret and bitterness. He hurts the child, because he refuses to play a major role in the child's life. As a result of his lack of commitment to the mother or the kid, arguments arise between the mother and father. Mr. LGHOB can't handle confrontation, altercation or being a good parent in that situation, so he moves on with the next chick leaving his child behind. He tells her, he loves her and the cycle starts again.

The Avoider

No phone calls, no text, no quality time, no connection. The avoider is the baby daddy that refuses to communicate with his child or with you. He will avoid y'all by any means necessary. Mom calls, no answer! Child calls, no answer! That's the game the avoider plays and he plays it well. The avoider refuses to understand the importance of communicating with his kids. He disregards their emotions and continuously lets them down. The kids have even memorized his voicemail greeting because they have heard the greeting more times than they have talked to him. The avoider gives children false hope because he says things like, I will call you later or call you back and he never does. Leaving children waiting until the point of despair by the phone for a call that never comes. Ladies, this right here is not fair! It hurts children to be forgotten and it makes the mother pissed, to know her child has been let down again by someone she choose to laydown with. At this point the relationship between the mama and the daddy has probably become hostile because no good mother will sit silently while her child is continuously being let down. Now he avoids his kids in an effort to avoid their mom. The avoider has this out of sight, out of mind philosophy. As long as don't see them, his children are not his priority.

The Liar

Always making promises, he refuses to the keep. The liar is the baby daddy no one needs. He too brings in disappointment and grief. He is also known as the false promise king. Every time, he talks to the kids, he tells them that he is going to do something and guess what, he almost never comes through. Neither the child nor the mother can depend on this guy. He says whatever he thinks y'all want to hear or whatever sounds right. The liar is full of deception all the way through. He lies so much, he actually believes his lies are the truth. The Liar even expects y'all to believe his lies too. It is very difficult for a mother to deal with the liar because she knows his words are never true. She contemplates on cutting the liar out of the child's life over and over again because she is tired of her child being disappointed. However, she doesn't cut the liar out of the kid's lives because she doesn't want to further hurt them. Each time the liar, lies, he tears his child down and the mother is left with the task of rebuilding the child and making the kid smile. Ladies, the liar is not a baby mama's friend!

Mr. Super Baby Maker (a.k.a. The SBM)

He got 5, 10, 15, 20 plus kids, Oh My! Mr. Super Baby Maker is not to be slept with. He leaves a child behind him where ever he goes. And guess what, these ladies, he is impregnating are not hoes. They have just merely fell victim to his ring of baby making. He can't possibly adequately take care of all of these kids. Some he sees and some he doesn't. Some he provides for and some he won't or better yet, he can't because he is not even balling like that. His kids only get $12.50 a piece for their child support check. PLEASE AVOID MR. SUPER BABY MAKER!!! I know he is fine but it's for your own good. I know he's a great lover but with all that experience, who wouldn't be. Ladies, don't be deceived, another baby is not what he needs. As soon as he gets you pregnant, he'll move on to the next pretty young thing and leave you all alone with a kid who has 20 other siblings with different mamas in different cities. In some instances The SBM will have the audacity to tell a baby mama, that he couldn't possibly be the daddy. So, to court they go and guess what happens when DNA is used to establish paternity…you've guessed it, The SBM is 99.99% the daddy. Oh and I forget to mention the affect of not having a good daddy on your kids.

The Forgetter

He cannot ever remember anything. He always forgets and never remembers. Not a birthday, holiday, special occasion or special event in his memory bank. His favorite excuse is, "I'm sorry, I forgot." His favorite line is. "What did I miss?" The forgetter makes you want to stop inviting him to the kid's events. He never shows up and his absence shows that your kids are not his priority. How is it possible for a man to consistently forget everything? The answer is that he doesn't care because if he did, he would remember or at least put a reminder in his phone so he won't forget. The forgetter makes his kids feel alone, rejected and neglected. He forgets so much that they realize he never meant it, when he said he would come, would call or would be there. The forgetter, has good intentions, he means to do well. He says timing is just not his thing. He apologizes every time he fails and sets a new date with the kids that soon become another failed attempt to remember. However, there are a few things the forgetter never forgets, his boys, his money, his lady friend, his job and entertainment. You see the forgetter actually remembers a lot of things, just not y'all kids.

The Apologizer

I apologize for having to write this to you…but I must write it anyway. I apologize for never being there for our kids but I love them more than words can say. I apologize that you didn't receive your child support this month but I'm working on that so you and the kids will be straight. I apologize for disappointing the kids but know each day I'm trying to make a way. I apologize I didn't call last week and I apologize I didn't return our baby's text. I apologize for not picking Jr. up from school but I promise ill pick him up next. I apologize for that girl calling your phone but I told her to chill out with all that mess. I apologize for not helping you as much to raise our kids but I've been under a lot of stress. I apologize for getting you pregnant cause I never realized this would be the result of our unprotected sex. I apologize for being the baby daddy you hate to remember and want to forget. I apologize because I know I'm in the wrong but I ain't going to change. I apologize for always leaving you with the kids but YOLO! I am the apologizer and I apologize for approving this message!

Mr. Take Care of Another Man's Child BUT Refuses to Take Care of His Own (a.k.a Mr. M.I.A.)

"Whose child is that?" says the baby mama to the baby daddy. "That's my girl's child", replies the baby daddy. Mr. M.I.A. hasn't seen his own kids in months but he is actively playing daddy to another man's kid. Who does that!?! This man refuses to assume any responsibility for his own kids but yet he has become a full time dad to his girlfriend's kids. F.Y.I. if you are the girlfriend know that he really doesn't care about your kids, he is just being good to them so that he can get in good with you and keep you grinning. He cooks, cleans, shows up and provides for another man's child while leaving his own seed standing on the sidelines. Mr. M.I.A. ain't anything to play with; he is the baby daddy the kids always miss. He acts like he is not concerned about his own kids. Mr. M.I.A. acts as if the kids he made don't even exist. He goes above & beyond for another man's kid but complains about supporting his. He likes to play the daddy role in every home because he is a rolling stone. Mr. M.I.A. continuously lets his children down and at times flaunts the kids who mama his is with in their face. Be advised the Mr. M.I.A. is unstable in all of his ways so keep him away from your kids and out of your face! He has no sense of loyalty, responsibility or commitment. When he breaks up with a baby mama, he also breaks up with her kids. Leaving them on the sidelines as he moves in with the next baby mama chick.

The Holiday Daddy

This is the daddy your child only sees at Thanksgiving, Christmas, Easter and maybe Mother's Day. Guess what, he is absolutely okay with that. It doesn't bother him at all that he only sees his kids 3 or 4 times a year. He actually feels great about himself for doing that much. At first it is a struggle for the kids to only see their dad on these days but after a while they get use to it. The children are left to deal with their dad's rejection for the remainder of the year. Begging him to come spend time with them but he never reappears until the next holiday is here. They holiday dad is only interested in his kids, when its time to show them off for the holidays. He boast and brags on his children like he actually knows them or like he has actually contributed to their over all well-being and success. The holiday dad only provides for his children during these times. He takes them away from the mother for a weekend or so thinking that makes his absence from his children during the rest of the year alright. After the holidays have gone, the holiday daddy drops the kids off back at home leaving them, sad, rejected and alone over the months to come.

The Gifter

The gifter is the baby daddy that has it together financially. He has no problem providing financially for his children. He expresses his love and his commitment to his kids through giving money and gifts (expensive and inexpensive). He thinks that as long as he is providing for his child financially, he is a good dad. Well …the truth is, his truth is not the truth at all. The reality is that his children are starving for his affection, attention and connection. The truth is that there are some things that money cannot buy. Gifts can never replace being in your dad's presence and truly knowing him. Through his giving of money and gifts, he teaches his kids how to receive but not how to give. He shows them that receiving gifts from someone is how they know they are loved. There is more to love than gifts giving. The gifter leaves his children without ever experiencing true intimacy with him. As the children grow older, they realize more and more that they never really knew the man that always gave them money and really nice gifts. Leaving the baby mama alone to pull all the pieces together to raise emotionally healthy kids.

Mr. If I Can't Be With You, I Can't Be With My Kids (a.k.a. Mr. Selfish)

This baby daddy bases his relationship with his kids based on his relationship with their mama. If he and the mama are in a relationship, he deals with his kids. But if he and the mama are not in a relationship, he does not deal with his kids. If he is on speaking terms with the mama, he will communicate with his kids regularly. But if he is not on speaking terms with the mama, he will not communicate with his kids. Mr. Selfish is unstable in all of his ways. His kids are not his concern but their mama is. He desires to control her, keep her from moving forward and block her every move. He consistently attempts to pop in and out of the baby mama and her kids' lives. His presence brings about an emotional roller coaster that leaves all people and children involved dazed and confused. This toxic relationship takes a huge toll on the kids and on the baby mama. Mr. Selfish doesn't believe in co-parenting, He wants all or nothing. Mr. Selfish does not know what he wants or where he wants to be however he does not want to be freed from the mother of his kids. In fact, in his mind, he has no way of separating his relationship with his kids from his relationship with their mama. Beware of Mr. Self because if he can't have you, he doesn't want y'all kids.

Mr. Oh Wait, I Forgot I Had Kids (a.k.a. Mr. Deadbeat Baby Daddy)

This baby daddy goes about his day-to-day life without ever thinking about or acknowledging his kids. He doesn't ever see them, speak to them or provide for them. He probably does not even believe that they exist although the paternity test has proven the kid is his. Mr. Deadbeat Baby Daddy is truly a deadbeat. He doesn't even attempt to be apart of his children's lives. He keeps moving forward with his life and never looks back at the woman he once laid with or at their kids. Mr. Deadbeat Baby Daddy leaves his children always wanting to know who he is, what he looks like, where he lives and why he never wanted them. Mr. Deadbeat Baby Daddy can sometimes be found with a suspended driver license, in the local jail, on billboards, having forced payroll deductions and confiscated income tax returns because he refuses to support he children financially. If you see this baby daddy on your street, point him out and tell him any boy can make a baby but a takes a real man to acknowledge and take care of his kids!
Note that your baby daddy may not fall into any of these categories and that is awesome. However some baby daddies may fall into one category while other may baby daddies may fall into several different categories. If you are a baby mama, I caution you to know exactly what type of baby daddy you are dealing with because you are stuck with them for the next 18 to 20 plus years. If you are dating a man with kids, I would caution you to observe how he treats the kids he has because if you get pregnant by him and you all break up, he will most likely treat your kids the same way, he treats the kids from his other baby mama. Lastly, if you are not a baby mama, stay that way. Being a baby mama is not a walk in the park. You really have to be careful who you have kids with because you will be stuck being connected to that person in some way, form or fashion for the rest of your life.

Chapter Five

The Good Baby Daddy

Ladies, having a good baby daddy isn't as rare as it may seem, they do actually exist. It isn't the materialistic things that he gives to you or to the kids that makes him a good baby daddy. He is a good daddy because he is emotionally connected to his kids. His dependable, responsible, consistent, considerate, caring, resourceful, providing and loving actions and attitude make him a good baby daddy. The task of being a good baby daddy may be difficult at times, but he will always go out of his way to put a smile on his family's face. Regardless of the obstacles he endures, he is always prayed up and ready for anything and everything that comes his way.

The good baby daddy always remains cool, calm and collect, always has self- control and carries himself in such a positive way. His positive swag is so contagious that as time passes it begins to rub off on you. Maintaining his self- control is something that not only includes him controlling his anger and patience, but it also consists of him kicking any bad habits that he may have had in the past. The good baby daddy started bettering himself and his life when he found out you was pregnant with his child. He consistently strives to be a good role model for his kids and he doesn't do anything foul, out of order or questionable in front of them. The good baby daddy threw all of his childish ways out of the window and stepped up to become a man of his word.

It's easy for a baby mama to respect a man who has self-control and does what he needs to do to make sure that he provides for his kids in every area... right? He understands that you are more than just his baby mama, he sees you as the mother of his kids and as a woman. Not just any woman but a self-respecting, independent, classy, intelligent, ambitious woman who doesn't take any mess from anyone... including him. He puts you on a high pedestal and cherishes the good works that you do for the children you share, even if those good works have nothing to do with him. You're baby daddy has an emotional connection with you and the kids; it's something that no one else could understand, only you and him. It's the emotional connection that brought you two together in the first place. Now that you have kids, it has traveled on to them. The children feel connected to their dad and they know their value to him.

The good baby daddy has his children at the top of his priority list. He is always concerned about the well-being of his kids, regardless if y'all are together as a couple or just co-parenting. His love for his kids is evident in all that he says or does. He makes sure the kids know that not only can they come and talk to you in a time of need, but they can also come and talk to him about anything and they feel just fine doing that.

It's attractive when a man is there for his kids, when a man can raise his son the right way, when a man can be good to his daughter, and his daughter can live like he taught her to. Being connected to your kids and in tune with them is a big part in being a good daddy and I'm sure you don't have to remind him of that because he knows exactly what to do and not to do. The good baby daddy is emotionally attached to his children. The word "emotional" means to bring on strong feelings, the feelings may be anger, sorrow, joy, love or any of the thousands of emotions that everyday people might experience. The good baby daddy knows how to brighten up his child's day. I wouldn't say he's perfect, but he is a good baby daddy.

The good baby daddy made the choice to open his ears to listen and his mind to learn about his child, empathizes with his child, and then helps his child grow in every way possible. He takes advantage of teachable moments and uses them as opportunities to teach his kids important life lessons and build closer and stronger relationships with them. The good baby daddy creates meaningful opportunities to bond with his kids. He doesn't try to put on a show for others or flaunt his kids around however he does attempt to bond with his kids anywhere, any place and anytime. He realizes the importance of bonding and so he never takes any bonding experience that he gets with his children for granted. The good baby daddy also never puts other people or social events before his kids.

The good baby daddy definitely knows that life is what you make of it, so he lives for the moments he gets with his kids. One of your baby daddy's most instinctive joys may be learning and playing with his child. Teaching his little boy to share, or letting his daughter know that she is the most beautiful girl in the world every chance that he gets, showing his son his first car, or driving his daughter to cheer practice when he doesn't have to. The good baby daddy makes time for his kids. He is the one that does piggyback rides, or plays action figures, or dresses up for your daughter's tea party. The good baby daddy takes his kids to church. He feels comfortable being with his kids and being for his kids.

You feel safe when you leave the kids with the good baby daddy because he's just as good with the kids as you are. There is no wrong in his parenting style. You're baby's daddy plays a very pivotal role in the children's lives. He encourages the kids to do better in school, listens to you, works with you and not against you, helps with the kids extracurricular activities, help around the house, etc. He does exactly what a man should be doing, taking care of his family. The good baby daddy is very dependable. He arrives when he says he's going to. He does what he says he's going to do and doesn't back track on it. The good baby daddy is a man of his word.

Children crave love and security and the good baby daddy recognizes that and he strives to provide his kids with what they need. He understands that the promises he makes are meant to be kept and so he tries really hard to keeps them. Yes, things do come up and not every promise can be kept… I mean, this isn't Jesus that we're talking about here, don't get it twisted. But, in the event that he cannot come through, the good baby daddy has shown up enough times that those small and rare occasions can be quickly forgiven. Basically, the good baby daddy strives not to disappoint his kids. He sees that his children take his words seriously so he will move mountains to be there for them. Yes, the good baby daddy can be counted on!

When necessary, the good baby daddy, like the good baby mama, will go without so that their children won't have to. Kids that grow up with a good and dependable daddy often grow into people who can be depended on. They have seen a great example and they, just like their daddy, become reliable, dependable adults. The good baby daddy is devoted. His love for his children is never questioned – not by the child and not by you. He is there to support and encourage, to offer assistance and advice and to love and to listen. This doesn't mean that he doesn't ever feel impatient, angry or disappointed, of course he does, he's human, so when and if you see this side of him, don't blow up and throw stuff in his face. Encourage him and treat him with love and kindness. Despite the minor setbacks, he always makes a come back. After all, he is a good baby daddy.

Not only is the good baby daddy devoted to his family, he is also devoted to His Father, God and when a man has a relationship with God, he is powerful and influential and is going in the right direction. He always re-assures the kids that their relationship with God is the most important relationship that they will have and they believe him. This just amazes you, I know girl, I know. I feel the same way. He teaches his children right from wrong and encourages them to make good Christlike decisions.

The good baby daddy is responsible and refuses to place unreasonable expectations on the children. He knows that his child's life will be filled with pressures, from outside influences so he labors to help lay a solid foundation based on God with his kids. He knows how to help his children understand their desires, their capabilities, and limitations (how far they can go). He knows how to help them set achievable goals. The good baby daddy encourages his kids to meet their full potential but avoids being overbearing.

The good baby daddy is responsible with the kids and he is responsible with himself. He doesn't place unreasonable expectations on himself... Just as he can't take credit for all of his child's strengths, he also shouldn't have to carry the blame for their weaknesses. It's only fair. He realizes that a daddy's job is never done. He knows not to assume that once the child turns 21, or they have a college degree, that his work raising them is done. He knows that although it is important to encourage children to become financially and emotionally independent, it is also important to let them know that he cares and will always be there for them and that they are valued by God, their mama and by him.

The good baby daddy is a man of character, quality and integrity. He is dedicated, determined and dependable. He is stable and consistent. The good baby daddy is an asset to his children and his baby mama. Ladies if your not married, this maybe your future husband (but that's another book)! He is a provider and a protector and he refuses to neglect his responsibilities. He has his act together. The good baby daddy never has to be told what to do for his kids because he does it automatically. He is not perfect but he always does his very best. He officially has a grown man status. Co-parenting with the good baby daddy is a pleasant experience, which does not include mess, drama or confusion unless of course you bring it. Ladies, please don't mess up a good thing. The good baby daddy is a keeper in fact he is the star player on your team. The good baby daddy is the baby mama's dream. —"When I was a child, I spoke as a child; I understood as a child, I thought as a child: but when I became a man, I put away childish things."- 1 CORITHIANS 13:11.

Chapter Six

Child Support, Oh Really!

Ladies, we all know that raising children is not cheap. Kids are expensive and in order to provide your children with a good life, you must have some money. I'm not saying you have to be rich to be a good parent or to provide your kids with a good life but you do need money to provide for the basic needs of your kids. This chapter will focus on how to get the child support your child so desperately needs, how not to abuse child support, why child support is so needed and when should you seek child support through the legal system.

First of all, let's talk about what child support is. Child support is simply money that is given to the custodial parent (that's you) from the noncustodial parent (your baby daddy), or the parent who does not have full custody of the child or children. Child support money is paid to the custodial parent in order to help the custodial parent meet the financial needs of the child and the household that the child resides in. This support remains in effect until the minor child reaches age 18 or beyond depending upon the state the minor child resides in. It is best to check with your state's child support agency or a child support lawyer, so that you will know and understand your rights and how child support in your state will affect your child or children.

Now, that we have a good understanding of the meaning of child support, it's time to get to the full fledge bizzness or business for some (funny, huh?) of getting that money. As a baby mama you need to focus on making sure that you do all you can to secure weekly, bi weekly or monthly child support payments from your baby daddy. Some baby mama's will try to set up voluntary payment arrangement with their baby daddy. What I tried to do was to honestly look at how much I needed to take care of my child each month. Then, I basically divided that by two and presented that number to my baby daddy. This worked out well for a little while, however, he soon started to miss weeks of paying, then the weeks turned into months and so on. My baby daddy provided me with all types of excuses of why he could not pay the support money and these excuses soon got old. Personally, I feel compassion for baby daddy's who are struggling, but shoot; they still have a responsibility to make a way to provide for their child or children financially. Baby mamas do it all the time, we work minimum wage jobs to take care of our children and some of us have to work 2 or 3 jobs to do it efficiently. So, baby daddies who fall into this category (being a struggling baby daddy) need to step up and do what is right and do whatever it takes to provide for their kids. Don't let your baby daddy or anybody else make you feel bad for requesting money from him to help you take care of your kids. Ms. Lady, yeah I am talking to you reading this book, it took two people to make that child, and it takes two people to provide financially for that child. (snaps finger and flicks neck)

Now I know your thinking, well I've tried to make arrangements with him and it didn't work. He wasn't consistent and he didn't keep up his end of the deal leaving me to cover all of the cost of raising our kid. So, this is what you need to do and make sure you read this very carefully because your child or children's financial well-being depends on you making sure that you do all you can do to secure financial support from your baby daddy. First, try effectively communicating your concerns about child support payments with your baby daddy, if he's willing to listen. Before that conversation, make up in your mind that will not beg him for money or argue with him about money. Together try to come up with a workable solution that is satisfying to both of you, give him one more chance to pay voluntarily. Now, if you and your baby daddy can't come into a peaceful agreement on a workable resolution to the child support issue then you need to go on ahead and file for court mandated child support. And don't let anybody make you feel bad about it and don't let your baby daddy talk you or guilt trip you out of it! Go ahead and contact your local division of child support services, they will be more than willing to help you and your baby daddy reach a child support agreement without the drama.

In this day and time, depending on the state you are in, child support can be filed for online. All you need to do is go online, type in child support office in your state and the website should be listed. If not, you can call your local attorney general office or local child support office to obtain information into how to obtain child support though the courts. Basically, if you can file child support online, you can just fill out the information for the custodial parent, because you are the parent who has full custody of your minor child. Once again, depending on the state that you reside, the process of after submitting your application could be short or lengthy. Just make sure after you have filled out the application, you jot down any contact information, so that you can call a caseworker to discuss the application process and get updates on the progress of your case. Once the application process is completed all you can do is just wait patiently until a caseworker contacts you or you get something in the mail. Make sure you are ready to present your case, because some men try to play the, I don't think the baby is mine trick. If so, most states do offer the non-custodial parent a paternity test for free or for a small fee. Just make sure you got your stuff in check and know for sure he is the baby's daddy. In most circumstances, if the baby daddy signed the birth certificate, a paternity test won't be used or offered, because the baby daddy has already claimed the child as his. But that don't necessarily mean he can't get a paternity test because I'm sure he will have his lawyer. So, just make sure that he is the baby's daddy to prevent unnecessary mess in the long run and embarrassment.

    If your baby daddy gets mad with you because you put him on child support and refuses to have anything to do with you or your child/children, then so be it. The reason why I say this is because your primary obligation is to make sure that your child is taken care of and that includes being sure your child receives financial support. There are too many children running around with inadequate things and living conditions because their daddy isn't doing all he can do to make sure that his child/children are taken care of. And there are too many baby mamas stressed out and overworked trying to make ends meet to support their kids on solely their own income.
Yes, it's great that he come by to visit and picks the child up,

but Ms. Lady, that won't pay for childcare, rent, clothing for your child, buy food, doctors bills, medicine, extracurricular activities and so on. Being a full fledge daddy, means being there for your child or children, taking care of your child/children needs, both physically and financially. It's time out for baby daddies just laying down making babies, and then moving on to the next chick, just forgetting about their responsibilities.

Ok Ladies! Now that your getting that child support money, don't abuse it! Child support isn't for taking care of you, the baby mama; it is for taking care of your child or children. So don't get mad at me, I am just telling you like it is. I hate to see a baby mama who takes their child/children child support money to take care of a man. If this doesn't apply to you, just overlook this and skip onto the next part, but if this does apply to you, keep on reading. Child support is not to take care of some grown man, who is more than capable of taking care of himself. If you insist on taking care of your man, then use your own money to do this or extra money after taking care of your kids. A real man doesn't expect for a woman to take care of him, he takes care of himself and tries to help his significant other. The only time you should be taking care of a man is if he is disable or sick and can't provide for himself. Otherwise, stick to using child support payments for your child or children only. Now, don't get me wrong, it's not a bad thing to help your man as long as he is helping you and you are working together to make your family strong and financially stable. Grown men are very capable of taking care of themselves and if they aren't this may not be the right relationship for you. Now, that's another entirely different topic that I'll save for our next book, so let's move right along.

One more thing before I move on, I have to mention baby mama's who try to take advantage of the child support amount. We know we need to get all that we can get, however, take it from me if you want to maintain a great relationship or beneficial relationship with your baby daddy, let's try to keep the payments fair. Don't expect your baby daddy to take care of you and your other children if they are not his unless he volunteers to do this. Try not to call your baby daddy for extra money when you know you just got a payment or you don't really need it. Don't be trying to blackmail your baby daddy either, for example, threatening him with increased payments if he doesn't do something for you or because he has a new girlfriend. Ladies, lets grow up and realize that if you two broke up, obviously things between you two weren't working out, so let him have his new woman. There are plenty of saved, handsome, mature, reliable, dedicated, sensual and good-looking men out there. Let's move on ladies!

I have heard some men say, "she don't need no child support, she just uses it to get her hair or nails done." Baby daddies are you kidding me? Child support is needed to take care of the children and to make sure they are provided for in the most beneficial manner. So, women the next time your baby daddy says that let them know this and tell them Shay told you to say it. I am so sick of hearing these lame brain excuses for why some men don't want to pay child support. Baby Mama if you want to get your hair and nails done, do that, just make sure your child/children hair and etc. are taken care of. When your child or children look tight, you are tight and you also deserve to look as tight as you want to look. So be you baby mamma and as long as you are using that child support check the right way don't worry about immature comments from others, including your baby daddy.

Now, on to another serious issue ladies and that issue is when should the baby mama seek child support through the legal system? This is truly an easy question to answer and it all depends on how your relationship with the baby daddy is going and if he is willing to pay child support without going through legal formalities. When I say relationship, I am not talking about if he still is getting with you or whatever. I am strictly talking about if he is spending time with his child or children, if he is building a solid parent to child relationship, if he is respectful to you and if he is paying child support and being a supportive dad. If he isn't then you may need to let the courts handle your child support arrangements and visitation arrangements. The legal system can be a very positive step for baby daddies who refuse to take care of their child or children. It can also be a great thing when it comes to setting up visitation rights and handling other child support issues. Such as having medical insurance under the baby daddy's job, helping to pay for childcare and etc. The primary reason why baby mamas deserve to get child support is because we deserve the right to have our baby daddy's help with the financial support of our child or children. Child support is used to help purchase clothing, to help pay the rent, utilities, to help buy groceries, medicine and etc. for our children. So let's make sure that we baby mama's do what we need to do to take care of our children.

     Hopefully, for those who don't get child support this chapter helped to encourage you to seek child support. Because having additional financial help to take care of your children can relieve a lot of financial burdens and heartaches. It can also make things run more efficiently when dealing with child support issues and parental obligations with your baby daddy. Some child support agencies offer parenting classes and all sorts of programs to aid in building a positive father and child relationship. Finally, having financial support and support in general from your baby daddy can aid in building a more stable, solid and confident family as a whole. Just remember to be mature, responsible, and intelligent and take care of your bizzness. (I had to do it again) Now, you got all of that information and now what? Girl, go on to the next chapter that's what.

Chapter Seven

Horror Stories

You became the mother of his kid but you never imagined that things would turn out like this. Some days you feel dazed, confused, torn, used, rejected, neglected, misunderstood and subjected to following the unspoken baby mama rules. You've been mad and you've been irate. You've let your emotions drive you to an unsafe place where you have done things that could have caused you jail time. That is, if you got caught! If truth were told, almost all baby mamas have been there right with you, living in a baby mama horror story. What you are about to read are real life stories of women just like you who had to endure the pain and overcome the struggle that being a baby mama can bring. The characters are fictional but as you read on you will see that you've heard it all before and the situations are the same.

Kelly and Mark

Kelly and Mark met about 7 years ago in Los Angeles, California. Kelly had just relocated to L.A. when she met Mark one afternoon at the pier. Mark was this fine, light skinned brother; nicely build, a good job, no children, respectful and dedicated. So Kelly thought she had found the perfect match for herself, after all she was educated, had a decent career, pretty and had it going on. Mark asked Kelly for a date and she accepted, and afterwards the two were inseparable. However, about a year later Kelly found out that she was pregnant by Mark, they were so happy and started to make plans for their future together with a child. Throughout the pregnancy, Mark was the caring, loving and supportive fiancée any women would love, but after little Mark was born things changed for the worst. Mark began to stay out late at night, other women were calling him, he ended up getting on drugs, he lost his job and he started to act violent toward Kelly. Kelly put up with his behavior for 2 years and things just got worst. Finally, after speaking with a relationship counselor, Mark decided to get help and checked himself into a drug rehab program and a domestic violence program. Both programs lasted for a couple of months and Mark and Kelly's relationship appeared to be improving. Mark found another job, stopped doing drugs, stopped being violent toward Kelly and supported his family. But the one thing Mark didn't stop doing was sleeping around with different women and Kelly found this out the hard way. Several months after Mark completed the programs, Kelly started to notice strange things about her body that wasn't happening before, and so she went to her Gynecologist to get a checkup. To Kelly's surprise she had contacted two STD's, Chlamydia and Genital Herpes. Kelly was so distraught about this and immediately called Mark, but he didn't answer his phone. When Kelly arrived home Mark was there, he had made a candlelight dinner and had planned a romantic evening for the two. But his timing was off, Kelly walked through the door, asked Mark about their child and told Mark it was over. Mark was hurt and didn't understand why Kelly wanted it to be over, so he kept trying to console Kelly. Finally, Kelly blurted out to Mark, "You gave me Herpes and Chlamydia, now I am messed up for life." Mark insisted he wasn't playing around anymore and he didn't have any diseases. Kelly threw Mark out and wouldn't take him back, no matter what he said or did. Eventually, Mark was diagnosed with Genital Herpes and informed Kelly of this. Kelly became even madder and refused to have anything else to do with Mark. The two continued to take care of little Mark and continued on with their life. However, the emotional toll was so overwhelming for Mark, because he couldn't stand loosing Kelly forever and he committed suicide six months later. Kelly was devastated and couldn't understand why Mark would end his life. Afterwards, life for Kelly became difficult; it was a real challenge trying to take care of a child in L.A. alone. She missed Mark and felt guilty for not standing by him. Little Mark became sad, because he missed his dad and didn't understand why his dad was taken from him. One evening Kelly became so depressed, that she took an entire bottle of sleeping pills and never regained consciousness. Little Mark found his mom dead on the living room couch and he cried so loud that Kelly's neighbors heard him. Little Mark didn't have a daddy or mother now and his life would be empty from that day on.

Keona, Lee and Connie

Keona and Lee were dating on the side because Lee was married to Connie and they had a child together. Keona believed in fairytales and thought Lee was her knight and shining amour. She did everything she could for Lee and thought he was doing everything for her. They would spend romantic evenings together and do so many things together. Lee would tell Keona, he was going to leave his wife and she believed him each time. After two years of playing the mistress Keona ended up getting pregnant for the first time, Lee was furious and convinced Keona to have an abortion when she was two months pregnant. He was a really convincing guy and Keona would do anything to keep him happy because she didn't want to lose him. After the abortion, Lee and Keona continued on with their secret relationship, he showered her with gifts, trips and even a home. But he never divorced Connie, his wife and Connie never realized her husband was cheating. A year later Keona found out she was pregnant again, this time she had made up her mind that she would keep the baby no matter what Lee said. Keona told Lee and he pretended like he supported her decision because he realized the pain the last abortion caused her. But, really Lee didn't care at all about Keona's feelings or about the love child she was caring. All Lee was concerned with was keeping Keona and the baby a secret from his family, which he did for years. Lee and Keona agreed to keep their baby a secret from Lee's family until he got a divorce in a few months. Those months changed to years and ten years later Keona was still playing the role of mistress. Lee began to stay away from Keona a little more each week and eventually broke off the relationship. Lee stopped seeing their child, he stopped supporting his child and Keona and disappeared altogether. Keona filed child support, but she wasn't successful because Lee was a liar. Lee used a fake name, fake birthday an all and he was nowhere to be found.

Keona had realized she was an idiot and should have taken the time to find out about her supposed to be man. Keona and her child were left homeless, with limited income and without anywhere to turn. Keona's child didn't have her daddy anymore and life as she once knew was over. Keona realized that Lee was never hers and she was playing with fire the entire time. While Lee was with his wife, Connie and children in another city living like the perfect family.

Veronica and Marcus

Veronica and Marcus are the classic boy meets girl couple. From the moment Marcus laid eyes on Veronica in high school, he knew that he wanted to make her his girlfriend. For months Marcus pursued her, conveniently positioning himself in her path. Until one day, he got her attention. Marcus showed Veronica things that she had never experienced before. He was exciting, caring, attentive, handsome and charming. Marcus was easy to fall in love with and hard to forget. The beginning was beautiful, like a dream come true. Veronica fell deeply in love with Marcus and although she vowed to abstain from sex until marriage she lost her virginity to him because she knew in her mind, he would be her husband. After the moment she had sex with him, everything changed. Marcus wasn't the same, he was no longer the innocent young man she fell in love with. He was living a double life; he had girlfriends on the side. He had habits that didn't make sense but still Veronica stood by him because she loved him and she believed he would become her husband. During the college years, they were off and on because he would basically come and go in her life as he pleased. He would manipulate her and hurt her from a distance with lies, foolishness and not to mention his other women. Marcus was a mess and his mess left Veronica in a state of rejection and depression. Veronica became a mess and for a moment her life was out of control. She began starving herself to the point of death as she lived with the pain and regret of giving her self away to someone who really didn't care. As time passed, she came out of depression and was able to move forward in her life but although Marcus was no longer physically there, he still held a place in her heart. What she didn't realize that when she had sex with Marcus, she and Marcus created a soul tie. They were still connected. Five years later, Marcus appeared on the scene again and guess what….they missed each other and picked up right were they left off. Kissing, hugging, touching, feeling, you know what came next. At the time they were both involved with other people, but they didn't care. The openly dated each other with out even considering how much they were hurting their significant others. They spent every free moment they had together, selfishly enjoying each other as they were enjoying themselves. They didn't care who they hurt in order to be together. Nothing and no one else mattered to them but them. One night Veronica and Marcus met up at their high school parking lot, yes they were creeping! They both wanted a way out of their current relationships and they wanted to secure their relationship with each other. Marcus asked Veronica to have his kid. They both agreed that having a baby would be the solution to their problem. They thought a baby would make their current mates leave them alone and free them up to be together. So they got busy getting busy and guess what…Veronica got pregnant. Marcus and Veronica were so connected that Marcus knew Veronica was pregnant before she knew. He called her one night and told her he had a dream that she was pregnant and advised her to take a pregnancy test. He was so excited. Veronica took the test the next day and sure enough she was pregnant. They were now both excited and anticipated the sex of the baby. Marcus was so connected with Veronica and the unborn child that he dreamed about the sex of the baby and knew it was a boy even before the doctors. Sure enough, when Veronica got her ultrasound it revealed that they were having a boy. Veronica's pregnancy was the worst. She couldn't keep down food, had morning sickness at night, was constantly spitting, sore, swollen, had bad heartburn, was miserable and constantly in and out of the doctor's office. Through it all Marcus was missing in action. He may have attended three doctor's visits during the entire pregnancy and it was his idea to have the baby. Marcus was present at the birth of his son, but it wasn't the Marcus, Veronica fell in love with. He was cold, mean and awkward towards his lover who recently became the mother of his child. He put on a good show in front of Veronica's relatives but after they were gone. Marcus was back playing hoe games again. He got back with his other girlfriend and forgot about Veronica and that he had a newborn baby. He didn't change any diapers and he didn't fix any bottles. He hardly even visited his own kid. He never took the night shift and poor Veronica was stuck all alone to care for the newborn baby that Marcus convinced her to have with him. Veronica was left to do all of the work for the kid he wanted. Marcus barely brought things for the baby or paid her any child support. When she confronted him about his lack of assistance and provision for their baby boy, he would blow up on her like he was the victim and like he was actually taking care of his kid. Veronica fell back into a state of deep depression because she finally realized the mess she had gotten herself in. Now not only was she being rejected but her son was rejected and neglected as well.

Tiffany and Drake

Tiffany and Drake met in college, they started off as just friends. They hung out together all the time but one day they crossed the friendship line and became lovers. They soon started dating and every thing seemed perfect. Tiffany had been hurt before and Drake was her knight in shinning armor. They were inseparable, always doing everything together. One night while they were on a mini vacation, Tiffany had a dream and it was very vivid. She dreamed that Drake had a girl friend with long pretty hair. Now Drake never mentioned a girl friend at all to Tiffany and when she mentioned her dream to him, he laughed it off like it couldn't possibly be true. He reaffirmed her she was his only girlfriend. Tiffany listened to him but her dream was so real that she had to be sure that Drake was telling her the truth. So, one afternoon, she hacked into his email account. She was astonished at what she found, there was in fact another girlfriend and this girlfriend had a child. His email was filled with all kinds of pictures of her, the kid and him. The emails were very detailed. After Tiffany gathered all of the information she contacted the girl and she confronted him. He continued to lie to both girlfriends. It was a hot mess. He admitted to Tiffany that, the child was indeed his kid and Tiffany stayed with him. During this time he didn't spend time with his kid. Within months Tiffany found out she was pregnant. She contemplated abortion but Drake wasn't really down for that. He told Tiffany to have his baby and he would be there to support her every step of the way. Drake broke up with the other girlfriend and focused on Tiffany. So Drake and Tiffany moved in together and started a family, he left his other child and the child's mother behind and didn't look back. Drake didn't see his other child, didn't call his other child nor did he acknowledge his other child but he catered to Tiffany during her pregnancy. He was at every doctor's visit and he was home every night. He worked hard and provided for their new family. Once Tiffany had the baby girl, Drake was the perfect dad. He spent more time with the baby than Tiffany. He nurtured the baby, cared for the baby and took care of the baby's every need. But, his other child was never in the picture and Drake never attempted to have a relationship with his other kid. As the years passed, this began to bother Tiffany. Tiffany tried to convince Drake to develop a relationship with his other kid but he wouldn't listen. He always had an excuse as to why he couldn't have a relationship with his other kid. Tiffany would cry out to him and tell him stories of how it felt to come up in a single parent home but none of that moved Drake. He focused on their baby girl and continued to do things his way. When Tiffany and Drake's daughter was 4 years old, they finally truly separated. Their relationship had ended but they agreed that they would both continue to be good parents to their daughter. For the first six months Drake paid child support on time and continued to spend time with his daughter regularly but then Drake got a new girlfriend. Drake stopped paying child support and stopped spending time with his baby girl as soon as he moved in with his new chick. He avoided his daughters phone calls. He didn't talk to his daughter for months. Drake didn't even attempt to see his daughter, the daughter that he raised and loved. Tiffany was left to pick up the pieces of her daughters shattered heart. She watched her daughter grieve over a daddy that wasn't even dead and that broke Tiffany's heart. Her daughter would cry out for hours almost every other day for her daddy but Drake had moved on with his life and didn't care about the pain he was putting their daughter through. When Tiffany discovered that Drake's new girlfriend had a child and that he was taking care of another man's kid but denying his own, she was livid and hurt. She didn't understand how a man could do for another man's child and not do for his own. Tiffany tried to reach out to Drake on behalf of their daughter but nothing worked. Tiffany experienced the pain of watching her daughter hurt and she began to blame herself. One day, she remembered how Drake just turned his back on his other child for her. She thought to herself, this is a great tragedy because the same way he abandoned his other child, is now the same why he is abandoning the child he has with me. Drake was never committed to his kids, he was committed to their mothers so when he broke up with the mothers, he broke up with his kids.

Devon, Necie, Sasha and Jenny

Devon is a slim, sleek, handsome man who gets what he wants and when he wants it. Devon is Twenty-two years old but, he definitely doesn't act his age, he acts his shoe size. Devon is a sweet talker, he'll put flavor in your ear just so you will fall victim to his tricks. That's exactly what his baby mamas did. All seven of them. They were all tricked and manipulated. See, Devon is one of those guys that sleep around and thinks that he will never reap the consequences. He's wrong though, everything has a consequence, and the name of his first consequence is Necie. Necie is a woman scorned. She "hates" guys and refuses to talk to anyone who can't prove to her that every guy isn't the same. She thinks that she is untouchable and that no guy is worthy enough for him to get the "golden ticket". She thought that for seven years… but, those seven years of celibacy and the man global man strike went right out the window when she met Devon. Devon saw her at the local coffee shop and started deciding in his mind what he was going to do and what his first move would be. You see Devon wasn't a guy that was just down for a long-term commitment. He was one of those "Hit it and Quit it" type of dudes and that's exactly what he was about to do to Necie. He walked up to Necie; Sat down beside her, licked his lips, batted his eyes, and said, "Is this spot taken?" Necie said, "No, sit". See, Devon looked at her and she felt like Devon was looking into her soul. He was just that smooth. He looked good, smelled good, and had it going on. Devon smiled with those pearly white straight teeth and said "Good, what's your name beautiful?" Now Necie was used to this, she turned around and said "Why, you want my number, you want me to call you, Nah Nah playa, I know the game." Devon laughed a light laugh and responded slowly "no baby girl, I've just never seen a woman of your kind before gorgeous, and I had to know your name". You get my vibe; Necie forgot about her "Seven year Strike" and fell into

Devon's web of woman. Devon had plenty of women, but he made Necie feel like she was the only one and that she was the most important lady in his life. When I tell you that Devon had game, you better believe me, he had game. Necie started to find herself getting caught up in this guy. Calling him every day, texting him every hour, stalking his social networks. But, every time he came home, he gave Necie a kiss; a massage and you know the rest. Well, Necie ended up getting pregnant with Devon's child and all the while, Devon was messing with another chick. Her name is Sasha But we'll get into her in a little bit. Necie was happy he got her pregnant because she assumed that this would make him behave and stick around. Well guess what? It DIDN'T! Devon became aware of the news and he didn't change one bit. Matter of fact, he started staying at Sasha's house more often than usual. You can only guess what they were doing right? (I mean I don't need to spell it out for you right?) Necie got further and further along and Devon was in and out of her life. He was still sweet talking her though. Telling her that he would be there, making promises we all know he didn't keep, messing around with Necie, and Sasha. Doing the do with both of them and no protection. Necie ended up giving birth to Devon's baby girl and they named her Deanna. Deanna was the spitting image of her dad, it was almost crazy, but Necie didn't mind it. She was so wrapped up in this guy having no idea that he wasn't wrapped up in her at all. He was still quite the ladies man and ended up being a great dad to his daughter. He got it together, so everyone thought. Necie claims that she started to see improvement in Devon and he started spending more and more time with them like a family should. "What about Sasha", you ask. Sasha was still messing around with Devon not knowing anything about Necie and vice-versa. Sasha and Devon were a couple, and Devon was feeding her the same lies that he was feeding Necie. Having sex with the both of them. Devon and Sasha were "In love" and shortly after dating for 4 months and hiding this relationship from Necie, Sasha was pregnant. Devon, of course, made her feel like everything was amazing and he would be there. And when that baby came, Devon was there. He was also still with Necie. Juggling two women at once making them feel like queens. But Devon was very secretive and he was also still messing around with some of his other baby mamas. To make matters worse Devon ended up messing with another woman that he met at a car wash function. Jenny. Jenny was cute, Devon's type and he of course was a man that knew what he wanted. When he wanted some, he got it. Devon instantly was attracted to Jenny and Jenny was instantly attracted to him. The sexual attraction was strong and they began being intimate very fast. AGAIN, with no protection. They weren't in a relationship though. Jenny was very secretive and didn't tell Devon anything about her. Devon didn't care though, they were just messing around. Well, Jenny ended up becoming pregnant. Let me finish, Jenny lost her baby. They stopped communicating shortly after. Necie and Sasha were still in relationships with Devon. Devon started to not act like himself. He started loosing weight, becoming sick and tired constantly. Sasha started having the same symptoms and Necie lost 25 pounds in two weeks. Necie knew something was wrong. Devon knew something was wrong, they thought it was the flu. Devon took it upon himself to go to the doctor. Devon was diagnosed with AIDS. He went home, kept it to himself, he didn't know what to do. He acted normal and still was the ladies man. He was still with Sasha and still with Necie, Neither of them knew about each other, at all. Devon got sicker and sicker and about a year later, he passed away. He died without either of them knowing about one another. At the Funeral, Sasha noticed Necie had a daughter around the same age as her son, and went up to her and talked. They talked and talked and found out that they were both seeing Devon at the same time. They were surprised that Devon hid this from them for so long. Devon left a letter of apologies to his two girlfriends and his baby mamas saying he was diagnosed with AIDS and didn't want anyone to know. Necie's health was declining and Sasha was also. Necie and Sasha were both diagnosed with HIV.

Mike, Sarah and Trey

Sarah had a daughter named Sidney, with Mike when she was 20. Sarah is now 30 and she and Mike have been broken up for over 3 years. Sarah and Trey have been married for 2 years. Trey doesn't have any biological children but he takes care of Sidney, like she is his own kid. Mike is very inconsistent, he is always popping in and out of Sidney's life. However, Sarah never denies Mike access to his daughter. Mike is irresponsible; he can't keep a legitimate job for more than three months. He is an alcoholic and selling drugs is his profession. Mike is about that life and its no surprise to Sarah because when she met him 11 years ago, he was doing the same things. Mike always provides financially for his daughter, so money is never and issue. When Mike and Sarah were together, Mike had tons of other women and he didn't try to hide it. At the time, Mike didn't believe in marriage, so he refused to make Sarah his wife. While with Mike, Sarah was taken care of financially but she had a high price to pay for that security. Mike would often get drunk and fight Sarah verbally and physically. He would embarrass her publicly. Mike was very controlling. As the altercations between Mike and Sarah grew worse, Sarah realized that this was not the life that she had planned for her daughter or herself. Months after Sarah and Mike broke up a friend introduced her to Trey. Trey and Sarah hit if off instantly and had a great connection. Within a year of dating Trey proposed to Sarah and they were married. Trey was a good friend, a good lover and a good husband to Sarah and a good stable daddy figure to Sidney. Mike became jealous because Trey had taken his family. Mike began to cause problems as a result of his jealousy. He would get drunk and come to the couple's house pretending to want to see his daughter only to start fights with Trey. Sarah never intervened in their altercations. She never stood up for her husband, she just stood back passively, shaking her head saying Mike was just stuck in his ways. Mike would cuss Trey out and tell him to stay away from his daughter. When Trey was not around Mike would make passes at Sarah in order to lure her back into a relationship with him. He would tell her how much he missed her and how she would be better off with him. For a while Sarah resisted Mike. Trey worked off shore so he was away from home for weeks and sometimes even months at a time. As business picked up with the company he worked for, he was pulled away from home even more. His time away from home began to take a toll on Sarah and Mike's marriage. One night while Trey was away at work, Mike came to pick Sidney up for the weekend, and he noticed that Sarah was upset so he began consoling her. One thing lead to the other and the two were passionately having sex. Mike told Sarah, he didn't care who she was married to, and she will always belong to him. He told Sarah how much he missed her and how much he needed her in his life. Mike told Sarah he didn't care about Trey and he never will. For months, Mike and Sarah were back at it but now Sarah was committing adultery. All this foolishness was taking place in front of Sidney. Mike had stopped drinking. Trey was always at work so for a while he had no idea about his wife's infidelity. When Sarah tried to break it off with Mike, things took a turn for the worse. Mike threatened to expose Sarah and blackmailed her into continuing her relationship with him. This time Sarah couldn't get away from Mike. Mike would also use their daughter to keep Sarah's attention. When Trey discovered what was happening things spun even more out of control. Mike started back drinking heavily. When Trey confronted Mike, they got into a huge fight. Trey warned Mike not to come back to his house or around his family. For weeks, Mike stayed away but he was hurt deeply from loosing for the second time the woman, he thought he loved. Mike started drinking more alcohol more frequently to ease his pain. He would drink all times of the day.

One afternoon, he went to pick Sidney up from school, he had been drinking all day long. He appeared to be normal but something wasn't right. While he was looking in the rearview mirror at his daughter in the backseat, he saw her mother and a tear fell from his eye. He unknowingly ran the red light and Mike and Sidney were in a terrible car accident. Mike was instantly knocked unconscious but their daughter Sidney lost her life.

Steven and Lydia

For 14 years, Steven and Lydia have been in this off and on relationship. Lydia is one of Steven's baby mamas. For the past four years Lydia has tried to break away from Steven but something keeps pulling them back together again. Now from the very beginning Lydia knew or at least she thought she new that Steven would be her husband. However, Steven never treated Lydia right. Steven was a destructive dog with fleas. Steven controlled and manipulated Lydia. Steven was a deceiver, full of lies. At one point, he controlled her thoughts, actions, how she dressed, what she would eat and where she would go. Steven was abusive and he abused Lydia verbally and emotionally. Steven had a hold on Lydia that time, distance and pain couldn't seem to break. Lydia wanted to move on, she tried to move on but she could never truly get away. Steven always found her and lured her back into his web of deception and oppression. It seemed like every time Lydia took three steps forward, Steven would pull her six steps back. Lydia often felt trapped and jumped at any opportunity to sever her relationship with Steven. The separation of the two never lasted long. In the midst of it all, Lydia got saved and began to get her life together. Steven resisted the changes that were taking place inside of Lydia but the Light that was within her made Steven want her even more. Steven was selfish and he believed that Lydia was his property. He would call her and tell her things like, "I don't care what you say, you are mine and you belong to me". He would shower her with deceitful flatteries and give her false hope. He would pop up at her home unannounced and shower her with his fake love. He would even use his child as a ploy. Only getting close to his child to get close to the mother. The reality was the Steven didn't care about his kid. Steven even went to the extent of perpetuating like he was a changed man. He was going to church with Lydia, praying with her and the child and everything. For a moment Lydia believed that

Steven was her assignment, like God had placed her in Steven's life to draw him closer to the Lord. Lydia really believed that if she continued to be good to Steven and show him the love of Christ that he would eventually yield but in the process she started yielding to him. After all Steven was her baby daddy and she loved him. The reality was that Steven was just running game. Lydia knew she deserved more she wanted more but she continued to settle. Lydia understood that as long as she settled, she would never get what she truly desired a God loving, God fearing, good and faithful husband. So, Lydia tried even harder to convert Steven and change him into that man but he resisted forcefully.

Susan, Robert, Lance and Tonio

Susan is a loving, caring, sophisticated woman who takes care of business and her kids... ALL THREE OF THEM. Susan is "the fertile Mama". Susan met Robert first, and fell victim to his lies, deceit and childish games. Susan was so in love with Robert that she was willing to do any and everything for this man. He would lie to her, cheat on her and all the while, still make her feel like she was the number one lady in his life. Although she was not, he had her fooled and looking foolish to all of the people looking in from the outside of her relationship. She was being played and she didn't even know it. She felt like his queen, she even thought he would be bringing a ring to her soon; little did she know the only thing that she would be bearing was his child. Nine months later, Susan was having Robert's first son. Robert continued to tell her lies and you know, make her think that he would be around always, even when times got hard. He was there... for the first month. Robert was nowhere to be found after he got used to that child. Susan tried calling him, No answer. Susan tried locating him but Robert couldn't be found. She didn't know what to do, she was lost, helpless and a baby mama. A single baby mama with a broken heart. Robert Junior had his dad's last name but his dad was never around. Susan felt stupid for allowing this to happen she knew she was smarter than that. Susan went into a depressed state and ended up being shut out from the world. She allowed a man to get control of her thoughts, mind, body and spirit. Her life revolved around Robert and now that he's no longer in the picture, she doesn't know what to do or think about herself. All that she can keep thinking about is the fact that her son will be growing up asking about his dad and he will be nowhere to be found. Susan is thinking that she won't know how to explain her unhappiness to her son. She figures that she needs to get it together and just play both mommy and daddy roles. She is determined to be the best that she can be for the sake of her child and she knows that she won't make the same mistake twice. She was working two jobs and trying to juggle her jobs along with spending quality time with her son. She's miserable, lonely and vulnerable. She does everything in her power to not let her son see that side of her though. He shouldn't have to suffer. While she has time off, she squeezes in time to hang out with her son, she often hangs out at the park where women and men often see her display her love for her child. She usually doesn't speak to anyone and vice versa until one day, while at the water fountain with her son, a guy comes up to her and speaks to her. Now, let me remind you that her heart is broken and we all know what that means. Vulnerability at its best; this guy asks her what her name is, and even goes so far to ask about her son. Susan loves this, she's thinking, "Wow, he cares to know more about my son" She's thinking that most guys don't even take the incentive to ask about her son. They just want to get to know her. They talk for about an hour while her son plays. She looks over and realizes that her son is playing with a little girl. The guy points out to her that the little girl is his daughter. She's around the same age as her son and this just makes Susan glow from the inside out. They continue to talk about their lives and they get to know each other in this short time span. Susan then realizes that she got so caught up; she forgot to ask him for his name. He gives her a piece of paper, goes to get his daughter, and they leave the park. Susan goes to get her son and they leave. The whole drive home, she doesn't open the paper and she's freaking out because she doesn't know the guy's name. They get home and get settled and watch some television. Susan Puts Robert junior to sleep and then remembers that she left the paper in the car. She goes to grab it, comes back inside, opens it, and then reads it: Lance (280-555-5505). Susan and Lance start to call each other regularly, hang out and let the kids spend time together also. Susan is still very open from her last relationship with Robert, but she also knows that she won't let the same mistake happen again (Or so she thinks). Susan and Lance start to spend more time at one another's houses and end up realizing that they have true feelings for each other. A few months go by and Susan finds herself moving in with Lance and seeing that she's "In love". She's never felt this way about any man, not even Robert. She feels like she's one with Lance, she falls back into the same cycle that she promised to herself that she wouldn't. That all goes out the window for Lance though because he's "different" and she's special. Susan is spending all her time with Lance. Lance has a good job, a strong head on his shoulders, he's sweet, intelligent, gives her everything she wants and more. Lance even goes so far to tell Susan that she can be a stay at home mom. Susan is in paradise! She loves this; no guy has ever cared this much about her and her child. Susan soon finds herself pregnant with Lance's child. Another Boy. Lance is ecstatic (so she thinks). Lance is feeding her lies, and the whole time that Lance says he's "working", he's actually putting his "Charm" on another female. He doesn't love Susan like she thinks that he does. Susan starts to feel distant from Lance and Lance starts to show and be more belligerent about what he's doing behind closed doors. He starts to show the man that he really is. He was a wolf in sheep's clothing and Susan was too love struck to realize that. Months go by and Susan finds herself in Early labor with her son. All the stress from Lance really put a toll on her pregnancy and this really hurt her. Her and Lance's son was born at 36 weeks and 5 days. He spent one week in the N.I.C.U. This really took a toll on Lance and while he was in the hospital with Susan, he agreed to change and be around during his son's life. Susan was happy that Lance decided to make this life changing decision. She thought that he was going to be a better boyfriend and a great dad. Susan started to realize that after a few weeks went by, Lance was coming around less and less. Lance finally ended up coming home… WITH ANOTHER WOMEN. Susan got her kids, her bags and left. Lance didn't try to stop her neither. Susan was back to square one, a single heartbroken baby mama with two different baby daddies and two kids. Susan had no job, no stable place to live and no one to talk to. She was in the same position as last time. She couldn't believe that she fell for the same game twice. She didn't know what to do or how to think. Her and her kids ended up living in a shelter and she ended up getting a local job as a waitress. It put money in her pockets, but not nearly enough to take care of two kids by herself. She was lost, broke and confused. She ended up moving up to manager at her job and she made enough to move out of the shelter and into a nice little apartment with a stable income coming her way. She had no help from either of her kids' daddies. She did everything she could to make sure that her kids were fed and happy. It was harder for her this time around though. Susan worked and worked and soon she found herself becoming great friends with a fellow co-worker. Tonio. Tonio was young, had no kids, a nice car and a nice place. He was polite and bright. Susan wasn't dating though. No-way Hose'. She was not falling for the same game. Tonio invited Susan out to dinner and although she was reluctant, she didn't decline his offer. They talked, mingled and got to know each other better. They were only "friends" though. Susan invited Tonio back her place for a little "Night Cap". Oops! They ended up getting a little too comfortable with each other, if you get my vibe here. Tonio wasn't interested in anything more though. Tonio ended up quitting that job and leaving the state. Susan was once again, PREGNANT. She became the repeat offender, raising three children by herself!

Alexandria and Tremaine

Alexandria caught Tremaine's eyes when they were teenagers. Tremaine has always been a ladies man, but it was something about Alexandria that was enticing. Maybe it was her beauty or maybe he saw her as an unclaimed prize. Either way as time passed Tremaine and Alexandria started messing around (sexually that is). They were not in a relationship because Tremaine was in a relationship with some other women but Alexandria didn't care. Eventually circumstances permitted Alexandria to become Tremaine's main girlfriend. Alexandria knew that she was not his only girl but she accepted it and continuously fought with his other girlfriends to secure her position. Tremaine was a ladies man, having sex with every woman he encountered. Alexandra and Tremaine had a very exotic sex life. Eventually Alexandria became pregnant and what should have been one of the happiest moments in her life, turned out to be one of the worse. She was his baby mama but come to find out she was not his only one. Tremaine's other girlfriend was pregnant too. Both baby mama's carried their babies and their expected due dates were the same. However, the stress of the situation forced Alexandria into an early delivery. Her baby survived the early birth but life with Tremaine after that moment was never easy. He was an alcoholic, violent, couldn't keep a job, unfaithful and in and out of jail. Most of the time Alexandria was taking care of him. But knowing it all Alexandria still settled because she loved him. He pursued other women and dated other women in her face and she allowed it. The love she felt for him was blinding. But what she didn't realize that she and Tremaine had created a deep soul tie. They were connected and no matter how many times he rejected her, she stayed around and refused to walk away. And in those moments when she got fed up and tried to leave him, Tremaine came right back to her begging her to stay. Their relationship was mess. He promised to marry her but the marriage never came. He even put a ring on her finger but he didn't mean it, it was apart of his game. Alexandria was his down chick, she was always down for whatever, she stood by his side through everything even though all the things he was doing was hurting her. Eventually Tremaine began seriously dating another female while he was with Alexandria and while she was planning a wedding. Tremaine had another baby, disrespected Alexandria, hurt Alexandria and embarrassed Alexandria publicly but she still stayed. Alexandria took pride in being his main chick, so she continued to settle. She thought that as long as he continued to lay up with her and spend time with her, everything was fine. She didn't realize that she deserved so much more, a man that would really love, appreciate and respect her. A man that would provide for her spiritually, mentally, emotionally and physically. A man that would honor her, her children, her body and make her his wife. Tremaine didn't love her; she was convenient just like all of his other women. He only wanted to control her and keep her from moving on with anyone else. Alexandria was blinded. She continued to settle and Tremaine continued cheating, creeping, lying, deceiving and playing games. Days turned into weeks, weeks turned into to months, months turned into to years, 30 years that is. Tremaine never stopped playing games, he never stopped telling lies, he continued to openly be unfaithful and Alexandria never became his wife. She settled for less than she deserved and got stuck in a position that ate away at her entire life.

The good news is that your story doesn't have to end like these stories did. We've seen your struggle and we want you to know that things can change for you and your family for the better. However, that change must start within you. Forgive your baby daddy for everything, he has every done to hurt you and your kids. Choose to be better and refuse to allow bitterness to grow within you. Everything you've been through and all the hurt you've experienced through it all was only allowed to happen so that it could help you and mold you into the strong women you are today. Your pain is connected to God's purpose for your life and the lives of your children. Give God all of the broken pieces and HE will give you peace, rest, hope, freedom and joy. What the devil meant for your harm, God is working out for your good (Genesis 50:20). So take a deep breath and keep moving forward. You are stronger now than you were before.

Chapter Eight

Testimonies

There is a certain stigma that the baby mama title brings. In fact, most mothers don't want to be called a baby mama because of the stigma associated with the title. However every baby mama and her situation does not have to live up to the negative baby mama stereotypes. There are some baby mama's who have their lives in order and their family in order too. They don't keep up mess, drama and confusion. Their situation may no have always been what it is today but they've worked hard to keep balance and peace and it shows. Over time, they have learned from their mistakes and their situations have grown into the good situations this chapter will spotlight. Although the characters are fictional, the situations are familiar to us all. Keep reading and take a peek into the ideal baby mama's life.

Claudia and Jose'

Claudia and Jose have been together for nine years and have two children together. Claudia and Jose live together and planned to get married in the spring of 2011. When they first started to date it was a magical experience because the two got along so well. They had a complete understanding of one another and knew what it took to maintain a healthy, loving and respectful relationship. When Claudia got pregnant with their 2nd child, Jose was there for her throughout every step and he supported Claudia fully, taking on the responsibilities of being a father and husband before they got married. After their 2nd baby was born Jose asked Claudia to marry him and she gladly accepted his proposal. A year after the birth of their little girl Jose and Claudia tied the knot. They had a small wedding at the church the two had been attending since they started dating. A few months after their wedding Jose enlisted into the Air Force and got into some trouble and ended up being released from the Air Force with a dishonorable discharge. Jose started to drink and stay out late often coming home with the smell of perfume on him. Claudia tried to handle the situation the best that she could, but eventually she got fed up with Jose and kicked him out. Jose and Claudia and Jose remained separated for 6 months and things got even more difficult for her. At times she didn't have enough money to pay her utilities and had to seek assistance with paying them, while Jose was busy getting drunk and hanging out with his friends and women. One day Claudia received a call from the emergency room, Jose had been in a severe car accident. Claudia was devastated and rushed to be by Jose side. Fortunately, Jose recovered from his accident and found the Lord in the process. He and Claudia got saved and devoted their lives to the Lord, to each other and to their children. Jose vowed to be the best husband he could be to Claudia and the best father he could be to his children. Their family was intact because of the support of their church, friends and families. Today, Jose, Claudia and their 2 children are doing great, they have a very successful relationship and they now understand and know how to handle tough situations within their relationship when they arise. Claudia was a baby mama who had many struggles to get through and at times she believed it would never get better. Jose didn't understand what it took to be a good father and husband. He started off being the best baby daddy any woman would want, but he ended up being the problem husband and baby daddy most women want to get rid of. Eventually, Jose got it together and Claudia never gave up and the two pieced their marriage back together all because of their faith in the Lord.

Taylor, George and Nancy

Nancy and George got married 10 years ago. However, George came into the relationship with a little extra package; he has a child with Taylor his ex-girlfriend. When Nancy met George she knew she found Mr. Right, because he was everything she envisioned a man to be and George thought the same about Nancy. The two hit it off from the start and were instantly spending a lot of time together. George told Nancy about his child with Taylor from the start and Nancy couldn't wait to meet his child. When the two met everything went perfectly, George and Nancy discussed the possibility of her meeting Taylor, his ex., Nancy agreed and the two met. At first Taylor was acting a little jealous and Nancy admitted that she really didn't feel comfortable around Taylor. Taylor would throw off hints whenever Taylor was around and this would make her very uncomfortable. The two got into a verbal altercation over the child and Taylor called Nancy every rude name in the dictionary. Sometimes, Taylor would try to act like George was still hitting on her and Nancy would start to second guess their marriage. She even threatened to take George to child support court because he wouldn't sleep with her again. One night when George took his son home, Taylor greeted him at the door with nothing but a robe on. She convinced George to come in to tuck his son into bed, and then once the child was asleep she tried to seduce George. However, George was use to Taylor's tricks and he resisted her advancements. It took two years after that incident for the trio to sit down to talk about their relationship and what needed to be done to make it all work. Taylor soon realized she needed to handle the situation like a mature adult for the sake of their child, the two women decided to get along and accept reality for what it was. Several years later, Nancy, Taylor and George are all enjoying the joys of parenthood. They all get together for the children birthdays and other special events. They now have a mature and respectful relationship and Taylor respects the fact that she and George are not together anymore and will never be lovers again.

Joanne, Steve, John and Carl

Joann is the baby mamma and wife, with 3 children by three different men. Most people would frown when reading this about Joann; however Joann and John got it all together for the benefit of their family. When Joann had her first child, she made a promise to herself that she wouldn't get pregnant again without getting married first. She tried to live up to that goal, but things didn't work out as she planned. After her relationship with Steve fizzled, she met Carl a few years later. He appeared to be the right man for her and they made plans to spend their lives together. They were together for 5 years until Carl was arrested and incarcerated for 2 years. A week before Carl got into trouble Joann found out she was 3 months pregnant. She panicked and couldn't believe that she once again chose the wrong route and gotten pregnant. Joann and Carl tried to make their relationship work while he was incarcerated, but it just didn't work. He constantly got into trouble and was arrested time and time again. So, they eventually decided to call off their relationship and once again Joann was stuck raising another child alone. Now, Joann was fed up and vowed to be celibate until she met the right man and got married. Well, six years later Joann did find the right man, and this man is her current husband John. John was the knight and shining amour that Joann dreamt of all of her life. He accepted her two children and decided to be the dad they never had. Joann and John got married and had children together, two little boys. Joann and John had discussed the issues regarding the two baby daddies and had decided to leave them out of the picture entirely, since neither one accepted the responsibilities of being a dad. When one of the children's dads decided to make a re-entry into his child life, John was the mature man to allow this to happen within certain boundaries. Joanne admitted it was tough but they eventually got through everything and the experience just made their relationship stronger. From the start John was a caring, responsible, dedicated, honest, God loving, and a very understanding man, who accepted Joann as she was. He took on the responsibilities of being a dad, when he really didn't have to. He was understanding of Joann and her children and he did what he was led to do because he loved his family. Today, Joann and John are still married, with four children and they are living as a complete and happy family.

Zoe, Rick and Lindsey

Zoe and Rick have been in a serious relationship for over three years. In the beginning of their relationship, they had a daughter. Before being in a relationship with Zoe, Rick was with Lindsey. Rick and Lindsey had a son. The situation between Zoe, Rick and Lindsey was rocky in the beginning. The two baby mamas were always competing with each other and battling for Rick's attention and love. At that time Rick wasn't innocent. He was with Zoe but he was still leading Lindsey on. Making Lindsey believe that they would be together as a family and they he would leave Zoe. Rick traveled back and forth from Zoe to Lindsey for over a year playing house in whomever home he was in. For a moment, Rick had the best of both worlds he had his ice cream and his cake. The two baby mamas were so busy fighting against each other that they didn't realize that their real issue was Rick. He was the one keeping up the confusion between the two baby mamas because he refused to make a decision about whom he wanted to be with. As time passed, Zoe grew tired of fighting to keep Rick, so she sat him down and let him know that today was the day he either made a decision or she would decide for him. See, Zoe finally realized that Lindsey wasn't her problem, Rick was and so she confronted him. She made up in her mind not to spend another moment fighting and competing with Lindsey to win Rick. And guess what, that's exactly what she did. Rick finally decided that Zoe was the baby mama he wanted. All of the cards were placed on the table and Rick got his act together. He stopped leading Lindsey on and started being faithful and committed to Zoe. He tried to co parent with Lindsey but things didn't work out at first because Lindsey was hurt, bitter and lonely. She started using her son to get Rick's attention. She was hurt and since Rick hurt her, she wanted to hurt Rick. Lindsey knew how much Rick loved his son, so she refused to let him spend time with him. She wanted Rick to feel rejected just like she did. Months went by and Rick was still not allowed to see his son. Zoe was upset because she wanted her daughter to have a relationship with her older brother and she wanted Rick to be in his son's life again. One day Zoe decided to reach out to Lindsey in order to put an end to the foolishness. Zoe realized that it just wasn't right for their children to be caught in the middle of some grown folk's mess. Zoe and Lindsey met up for lunch they talked for hours and apologized to each other for the way that they had treated each other in the past. They both knew that they were not each other's enemy. They realized that they were both fighting to keep someone they both thought belonged to them. That day, Zoe and Lindsey forgave each other and agreed to work together to effectively raise their kids. They went into the restaurant as enemies but left out of the restaurant as friends. It was by the grace of God that this reconciliation had taken place. Zoe helped Rick get his relationship back on track with his son. Lindsey began to allow her son to spend weekends with Zoe and Rick. Soon, Zoe allowed her daughter to spend weekends with Lindsey and her brother. Over time Zoe, Rick and Lindsey became a blended family. They worked together as a team to raise their children effectively. Both baby mamas trusted each other with their kids and there was never any foolishness or animosity. Zoe and Lindsey learned how to work together and stick together and they also learned how to deal with Rick. These baby mamas learned how to encourage and motivate each other after they stopped competing. Zoe and Lindsey truly looked out for each other's child just as if the child was their own. Now the two children have Rick, Zoe and Lindsey to look after them.

Kesha, Kyle and Tina

Kyle is Tina's husband but Kesha's baby daddy. Kyle and Tina have been married for a year. Kyle and Kesha have two daughters together from their previous relationship, they were never married but they got pretty close to it. Kyle and Kesha realized long ago that they were better off as friends. Today, Kyle and Kesha have an awesome relationship as friends and parents. They have mastered the art of co-parenting. At one point their daughters were spending every other weekend with Kyle and Tina. However, the girls loved it when it was just them, mom and dad. Both daughters wished Kyle and Kesha would get back together again. At times the daughters were rude and disrespectful to Tina because they felt like she was trying to take their mother's place. They often lashed out saying things like, "she ain't my mama" and "daddy we don't like her". They refused to do anything Tina said and they refused to accept any correction that she sent their way. Tina was good to her stepdaughters and she loved them but they never treated her good in return. For months Kyle overlooked his daughters' behavior because he had them on such a high pedestal. When Tina brought it to his attention, Kyle came up with a plan. In order to keep down conflict Kyle just started to spend more time with his daughters at their mother's house and avoided when at all possible bringing them into his home. Kesha was still single! They began to do more family outings just Kesha, Kyle and their two daughters. Tina was always left out of the picture and after a while that started to bother her. Tina began to think her husband was cheating and getting ready to leave her to return back to his baby mama. After much prayer and months of holding back, Tina expressed her feelings and concerns to Kyle. She informed him that she was insecure about him spending so much time with his baby mama. Kyle assured her that nothing foul was taking place and that he was just being there for his daughters. Tina suggested that they all get together to discuss how to handle the situation with the girls because the current situation no longer worked for her. Kyle agreed with his wife and contacted his baby mama. This would actually be the first time they all got together to discuss the girls. Normally Kesha and Kyle handled things pertaining to their daughters on their own without Tina's input or opinion. Kesha, Kyle and Tina sat at the dinner table and discussed what was going on with their daughters. Tina assured Kesha that she would never try to take her place, hurt her daughters or bad mouth her in anyway and Kesha believed her. At the end of the conversation, they all agreed that it was time to talk to the girls as a family. During this family meeting Kyle, Kesha and Tina were all on the same page. The scolded the daughters for their manipulation and misbehavior and informed the girls that they will respect and honor their stepmother. Once the children realized that their parents were in this together, things improved. Kyle began backing up his wife and supporting her with his kids. Kesha, Kyle and Tina learned the art of parenting together. Eventually Tina developed a great relationship with Kyle's daughters. Tina would pick them up from school, take them shopping and spend quality time with them. Through it all Kesha, Kyle and Tina had become friends and enjoyed their blended family. Now family outings included Kesha, Kyle, Tina and their two daughters.

Dexter, Anna and Malik

Dexter and Anna met at a party and things started off fast for them. After their 3rd date, Dexter and Anna consummated their relationship and two months later Anna founded out she was pregnant. Anna already had a little boy, who was 1 year old. She got pregnant with him from having a one night stand with Malik, a 23-year-old pre-med student. So she wasn't too thrilled about being pregnant again and started to think about an abortion. But as soon as she told Dexter, the abortion idea went down the drain because Dexter wanted her to keep the baby. Anna was confused at the time but she did just what Dexter had asked her to do because she had fallen in love with him. Throughout her pregnancy Anna revealed that Dexter was by her side through everything. He was even by her side when Malik came back into the picture and wanted to spend time with his child. Malik took Anna through so much while she was pregnant with Dexter's child. He threatened to take her to court for full custody of their son because it was later revealed that he was jealous of Dexter and Anna's relationship. Dexter and Malik got into a physical alteration one time when Malik disrespected Anna in front of him. Dexter didn't like Malik at all but he tried to remain respectful because he loved Anna so much. Dexter was there and he stood by her side every step of the way. After the birth of Dexter and Anna's baby, Dexter asked Anna to marry him. She accepted his proposal and they got married a year after their baby's birth, the same year Anna and Dexter graduated from junior college. At first being married at such a young age was hard, Dexter had to work 2 jobs and had to put off going back to school. Malik tried to cause problems every so often or tried to brush up on Anna. Anna was tired from raising two children, trying to attend college and being a young wife. However, Dexter and Anna committed to one another and made up their minds to work hard to keep their family together and to be happy. They both knew it would be hard because they were both so young; however, they made a vow to make it work. Anna put Malik on child support and gave him supervised visitation rights, Dexter had a long talk with Malik and he agreed to stop hitting on Anna. Anna admitted that she had to threaten Malik with no visitation rights if he kept on creating problems and possible violent situations. Two years later, Anna and Dexter are still happily married; her baby daddy is still being responsible and sticking to their arrangement. Anna and Dexter are still working hard to take care of their family. Dexter landed his dream job and no longer works two jobs. Anna is employed part time and she is only two semesters away from receiving a nursing degree.

Clarence and Shelly

Shelly was thirty-two years old when she first met Clarence, who was thirty. Shelly wasn't looking for anything too serious at that time, she was just enjoying being a happy, beautiful, and independent woman in her early thirties. Shelly and Clarence met in a line at a local food store and little did she know that her life would be forever changed by this man. Clarence was a nice, average looking guy; Shelly really had no interest in him and really just wanted to be his friend. Clarence accepted that and asked Shelly for her number, too his surprise, she didn't decline. After the exchange, Shelly and Clarence really didn't talk that much. I mean Clarence called every once in a while but Shelly never once called Clarence. Months went by and Clarence ended up deleting Shelly's number out of his phone. Shelly definitely was up to part looks wise, but she made no effort to get to know him. Clarence was sick of making all of the effort. One morning while Clarence was lying in bed, Shelly decided to give him a call. Clarence was kind of resistant at first, but they ended up talking for about two hours and ended up having a great conversation. Shelly had more in common with this man than she thought that she did. Clarence asked Shelly if she wanted to go out for bowling that Saturday night and to no avail, Shelly said yes. Shelly and Clarence met up at the bowling alley that night around eight thirty and didn't leave until eleven. They ate, had some drinks, bowled and got to know each other a whole lot better. Shelly was amazed at how much fun she had with Clarence, Clarence knew that she was going to be a good friend of his. Clarence and Shelly left the bowling alley that night and talked every day until they saw each other again. Shelly enjoyed Clarence a lot and about three months after the bowling alley date, Shelly invited Clarence over for dinner at her house. Clarence made sure that she was comfortable with that and asked her if she was sure. Shelly was definitely sure that she wanted to see this man again and spend more time with him. Clarence went over and they had a great time. Clarence helped Shelly cook and even helped her clean up once they were done. Never once did Clarence make any sexual advance toward her, Shelly loved that. Clarence went home that night but, before he left… he gave Shelly a soft kiss on the cheek. Shelly was falling for Clarence but, she wanted to take things slow. Shelly was a strong and firm believer of not rushing into things, she believed that you have to build a strong friendship with a man before you get into a relationship with him. The two began to fall for each other. They spent every moment that they could together and always had the best time doing it. One night after dinner and a movie, Shelly told Clarence that she was too tired to drive back home that same night. Clarence was reluctant to let her stay the night because he too was a firm believer of taking everything slow. Shelly and Clarence played Cards that night, had some wine and talked about life. To Shelly, Clarence was perfect, and to Clarence, Shelly was perfect. They knew each other in and out, they loved each other and it took them a whole year to even realize that they could possibly be soul mates. Clarence and Shelly shared their first real kiss that night. Shelly never felt this way when she kissed any other man before, and one thing lead to another and they were having sex. The next day, Shelly kissed him goodbye and told him that she would call him. She didn't. Clarence tried calling Shelly but, Shelly didn't pick up. Clarence figured that he had done something wrong and he continued to call, text and leave her voicemails. A few weeks later, Shelly called him; Clarence was mad, but he loved this woman, so he talked to her. Shelly was pregnant and Clarence was SHOCKED! Clarence didn't know what to do, I mean, he had never had a child and he was confused. He told Shelly that he would call her back. Shelly thought to herself that she was going to be another single mom out here struggling with a child that has no daddy. Clarence called Shelly back and told her that he was going to work and provide for Shelly and his child. During Shelly's pregnancy, Clarence asked Shelly to marry him, She said yes! They had the perfect wedding. Shelly moved in and Clarence worked his butt off. He had two full time jobs, and bought another car for Shelly so that she could go where she needed to go. He bought Shelly everything that she needed on top of giving her money. He gave Shelly his debit card and told her to go buy whatever she needed for the baby. Shelly did just that. She was amazed. When the baby was born, Clarence stepped up even more. Clarence told Shelly that she didn't have to work; She could be a stay at home mom and raise their little girl. They named Her Aria. Clarence put food on the table, worked, bought Shelly flowers, cards gifts, and was an overall package. Shelly was head over heels for this man and Clarence felt the same way. Shelly and Clarence are now living the married life in South Carolina and they another child on the way.

Chad and Whitney

Chad was a ladies man. He learned the love of women from an early age. Chad was known for always having two to three women on his team. He was a playa; a pimp and some might even call him a hoe. For a moment in his life, he was making babies on every corner he turned. Chad was the worst, he was no good and low down, well at least that's what his baby mamas might say. Chad was already a baby daddy to two or three children when he met Whitney, but that's where his story will begin. Whitney was an innocent girl with a bright future ahead of her. She was beautiful, intelligent and pure. When Chad laid eyes on her, he knew he had to have her, sexually, that is. Before ever making his move on Whitney, he watched her from a distance as he came up with a plan to get in her pants. Chad was a ladies man, tall, dark, handsome and smooth. Chad moved in on Whitney in the blink of an eye. He talked a good game and feed her tons of lies. Chad got in Whitney's head and then she fell deeply in love with him. She believed that Chad was the one, so guess what….she gave up the goods to him. In fact, he was the one, the one to run away from. In reality, Chad was not the ideal candidate for her virginity but she was blinded by his deception and she could not clearly see who she was connecting with. Chad got Whitney pregnant instantly and she was pregnant with a baby girl. She named her daughter Layla. Layla was Whitney's first born but she wasn't Chad's first born. Eventually Whitney discovered that she was never Chad's only lover. He had two other ladies pregnant with babies on the way at the same time she was carrying Layla. Whitney was pissed and she was often found in battles fighting against Chad. One day Whitney even tried to take Chad's life. All along their beautiful daughter was caught in the middle of their strife. The situation between Chad and Whitney was pure hell but Chad loved his daughter, or at least, he claimed he did. His actions sure didn't show it. Chad rejected his daughter and for the next 26 years Layla never saw her daddy's face. The final separation between the three took place when Whitney and Layla moved to another state. As time passed, Chad continued to live his life with his other seven children. He lived a hard life with ups and downs, ins and outs. At one point Chad lost everything except for his relationship with his Heavenly Father. Over the years, he realized all the pain and frustration he put Whitney through and he deeply regretted it. Chad acknowledged his wrong to God. Chad prayed to be reunited with his daughter. He searched for her but he never could find her. He had heard some stories about her but he couldn't pin point her location. Time continued on and now his little girl was now a grown woman with her own children. Layla never really desired to know more about her mama's baby daddy, but a couple of her loved ones did, so she sent him a letter. When Chad received the letter, he instantly grabbed the pictures of Layla when she was a little girl and tears began to run down his face. Chad knew he didn't deserve to be in Layla's life but God had mercy on him and gave him his heart's desire. After 26 years Chad was reunited with his daughter.

God specializes in turning tests in to testimonies, just trust Him and pray about your situation. Faith, love, hope, peace, prayer, forgiveness, perseverance, determination, honesty, work and maturity are all parts of a baby mama testimony.

Chapter Nine

Baby Mama 101

Things Every Baby Mama Should Know

Being a mother is very rewarding but the demands of co-parenting with a baby daddy can make parenting a difficult task. Oftentimes baby mamas are left to carry the burden of full time parenting without any spiritual, emotional, physical or financial help. Women are considered the primary caregiver in the home. In most cases, the baby mama has to be the spiritual leader, caregiver, provider, and play both parents role in the home. Now more than ever, women are expected to do it all. The good news is that baby mamas have been successfully raising successful children and maintaining peaceful homes for decades. The struggle of being a good mother to your kids while being a good baby mama is very real but with Christ it can be done. Keep reading and you will find a few things every baby mama should know.

1. *Your help and your strength come from the Lord!*

Just face it head on, you cannot be a good parent to your kids on your on. The demands of parenting cannot be effectively met without the help of the Lord. The burden is too big to carry by yourself but the good news is that the Lord will carry the burden for you and help you along the way. Disappointment often comes when we expect people (ex. Baby daddies, relatives, friends, systems, etc.) to help us raise our kids and that help never comes. Disappointment also comes when we expect baby daddies to do their part and they refuse to do the very things they are supposed to do. Know that God is more than able and ready to help you successfully raise the kids that He has given you. So whenever you need help or strength on this journey of motherhood, pray to God for it and watch Him bring you every resource and person that you need to be a good baby mama.

2. *Know who your dealing with!*

Its very important for baby mama's to know what type or types of baby daddy they are dealing with. The type of baby daddy you have will determine the type of struggles you will have to face as his baby mama. Pay attention to how he operates so that you can be strategic about how you deal with him. Refuse to allow yourself to expect more from him that his is capable of giving. When you realize who you are dealing with, you will put yourself in a better position to co parent with him.

3. *Your primary responsibility is your kids!*

You are a baby mama, so you don't have time to be concerned with a grown man. Focus on your kids and making sure that you are being the best parent that you can possibly be to them. Take that same energy that you use to be bitter at your baby daddy and use it to be better to your kids because they need you.

4. *Keep the peace between you, your baby daddy and his wife or girlfriend!*

Baby mamas have a bad reputation because it is said that they keep up mess, drama and confusion. Don't let that be you! Don't allow yourself to go to war with him, his wife or girlfriend. You are more than mess, drama and confusion. You are the mother of his kid or kids. In fact, you are a good mother, so let that show in every thing that you do. Keep your haters quiet by letting your goodness speak for you. If he has moved on, let him keep moving but don't prevent him or hinder him from being a parent to your kid. Remember its not about you, him or her, its about your kids. Refuse to entertain drama, fight all your battles on your knees in prayer and watch God work everything out in your favor.

5. *Cope with the foolishness!*

There is a certain level of foolishness associated with being a baby mama. Don't avoid it, deal with it and deal with it effectively. If God has allowed you to be a baby mama, I am convinced that God has already placed on the inside of you everything you need to cope with the foolishness. Dig deep, it's in you! Refuse to allow difficulties to defeat you and make life difficult for you and your kids. Pray to God and listen to his directions. God will give you peace instead of chaos, joy instead of sorrow, security, rest and hope.

6. *Be consistent with your kids in spite of their inconsistent daddy!*

You cannot force your baby daddy to be consistent with your kids, but you can be consistent. Strive to be consistent in everything that you do. Inconsistency leads to failure and consistency leads to progress. Don't allow your baby daddy's inconsistencies to affect you. Continue to consistently do what's best for you and your kids regardless of what your baby daddy chooses to do. It is what you consistently do that will make a huge difference in the lives of your kids.

7. *Teach your kids how to respect, honor and obey their daddy in spite of his flaws!*

This one is easier said than done but it must be done. Its easy to tell your kids how horrible their daddy is, how he refuses to take care of them, refuses to provide for them and how he doesn't love them and can't tell them what to do but you must never do that. Regardless of what he does or does not do, he is still their daddy. The Bible teaches us to honor our mother and father (Exodus 20:12 & Ephesians 6:2), it does not say honor only our good mother and good father. Which means it doesn't matter what type of parent your baby daddy is, God said honor him and that's what you teach your kids to do. In fact when you teach your child to respect, honor and obey their daddy, they will be in a better position to respect, honor and obey God and you. Also, when your baby daddy consistently experiences how good his kids treat him in spite of how wrong he does them, that will in itself convict his heart and cause him to want to do better for his kids.

8. *Never downgrade your baby daddy or talk negative about him especially in front of his kids!*

This goes along with number seven but for reiteration purposes if its not nice or helpful don't say it (Ephesians 4:29). Also, your baby daddy will never become a good baby daddy if you keep talking about how bad of a baby daddy he is. When you talk about him maximize your conversation about his good qualities and minimize your conversation about his bad qualities. Talking bad about him is not going to make him or you any better.

9. *Refuse to argue with your baby daddy, especially in front of your kids!*

Kids don't understand when adults argue and young kids often think that it's their fault y'all are arguing. Well it's not their fault and children should not have to deal with all of that. It negatively affects children when they see their parents lashing out at each other, so stop it. If you can't talk about it calmly then don't talk about it at all. Arguing won't change any thing; in fact in most cases it just makes the situation worse for everybody involved. The decisions that are made during arguments are the decisions that people often regret because they only made that decision because they were angry. Refuse to allow angry emotions control you and pull you into an argument. If your baby daddy wants to argue, let him argue by himself.

10. *Avoid disappointment at all cost by keeping your hope in the Lord!*

The truth is, your baby daddy will disappoint you. In fact, in life a lot of people will disappoint you, so get over it. Disappointment hurts so to avoid it, keep your hope in the Lord. God is the only one that has promised to never leave you or forsake you (Deuteronomy 31:6). Keep your expectation in God and not in human beings. God is faithful and capable of meeting our expectations every time. Don't set yourself up for disappointment by having expectations for your baby daddy that he cannot meet because as soon as he doesn't do what you expect him to do, you will be disappointed and mad. Expect from God not man!

11. *Teach your kids how to look to God as their father & show them how to trust in Him!*

God is our father and it is so important that our kids know that (Psalm 68:5). God is the ultimate provider of all of our needs. Teach your children that God is their father, show them how to spend time with God, how to pray to God and how to love and praise Him. Help your kids start and build a healthy relationship with their Heavenly Father.

12. *Teach your kids how to pray!*

Prayer is simply talking to God. Prayer is powerful and it changes things. It is so important for baby mamas to teach their kids how to go to God on their own in prayer. Pray with your kids everyday and let them know how important it is to call on Jesus and talk with Him during the day. Ain't nothing better than having some praying children because when you can't pray, they will pray for you. Teach your kids how to pray for their daddy, too. God has the power to change him and transform him into the baby daddy you desire and the parent they need.

13. *Forgive! Be better & not bitter!*

No matter how bad you and your kids have been hurt, you must forgive. Make up in your mind to never withhold your forgiveness from anyone. The Bible teaches us that if we fail to forgive others, God will not forgive us (Matthew6: 14-15). I don't know about you but I need forgiveness from God everyday! When you withhold forgiveness, you're only hurting yourself because unforgiveness leads to bitterness. Bitterness will rob you of your peace, freedom, joy and happiness. Choose to be better and not bitter. Free yourself and your children by always choosing to forgive.

14. *You can make it, even if child support never comes!*

God will provide for you and your children with or without a child support check. I am a single mother of two with one income and no public assistance, and my household (which includes me and my children) lacks nothing. This is because I trust God to meet all of our needs and pay my tithes faithfully and guess what God does it every time. Paying your tithes ensures the blessing on your life and in your finances (Malachi 3:10-12). When you trust God with your money, you are going into to business with Him. God is the best business partner you could ever have. He always makes good investments and He always produces a good return. God will bring you out of debt and move you into the land of abundance with or without that child support check! You don't have to beg your baby daddy for money and go through hoops, hurdles and arguments just to get it. Trust God and ask God, He will bless you and your kids and there will be no sorrow added with it (Phillippians4: 19, Proverbs10: 22)

15. Budget, save and maintain!

A budget is just a plan for your money. People who fail to make a plan with their money often plan to fail at managing their finances. Being a baby mama does not give you an excuse to be broke and in poverty. Being a baby mama gives you a reason to keep yourself together financially. You need you to be financially free so that your kids can grow up and be financially free too. Nobody wants to be in bondage to bills. Whether you realize it or not your kids will most likely inherit your financial habits, so give them a good example to follow. At times it is hard to save when your income alone has to meet everybody's needs but with God it can be done. Be purposeful about saving for you and for your kids. Open up savings accounts for everybody in your house and put something in it every month, even if its only $5. Teach your kids how to pay their tithes, budget and save. Help them learn how to make good financial decisions and don't let them just buy things just because they want them (especially if you are not rich). When their dad gives them money help them to manage it wisely. A fool spends everything she has but a wise woman budgets, manages and saves.

16. Be willing to give and receive!

The Bible teaches us that whatever we give, we shall receive (Luke6: 38). If you are a giver, you will be a receiver. Don't give any kind of way, be a cheerful giver. Refuse to be a hoarder and hold on to everything just because you're stingy (Proverbs11: 24-25). Give, give, give! If you can't use it, don't use it, don't need it, don't want it or see somebody in need of it, give it away and let it be a blessing to somebody else. In turn, God will bless you for blessing others. The more you give to others, the more you will receive. Build a culture of giving in your home and teach your kids how to give freely.

17. Laugh and don't cry!

As a baby mama, there are many times, when you feel like crying yourself to sleep because of the things that you have to endure. Don't let your tears be the end of your story. Remember that weeping may endure for the night but joy comes in the morning (Psalm30: 5). Don't let the hurt, frustration, or disappointment, anger or pain break you. Allow it to make you into a better woman, mother and friend. Regardless of what time of day it is, it's your morning time! Shake off the disappointment, frustration, lack, anger or pain, smile and laugh out loud! While you laugh remember this one truth that God is working all of what your going through out for the good of you and your kids (Romans8: 28).

18. Don't be a hater or hang with haters!

Being a hater will make your situation worse. Refuse to hate on others because of their accomplishments or foolishness. Be satisfied with who you are and what you have. Don't compare yourself, your kids or your baby daddy to anybody else cause that's where you will allow foolishness to invade your life. Be a congratulator and a motivator, encouraging others while also encouraging yourself. Refuse to be that stereotypical baby mama you hear about in rap music and r&b. Be the baby mama who is an asset to her kids and her baby daddy. Be helpful and resourceful. Keep those other hating baby mamas out of your face because misery loves company. If their situation is messed up, they will want yours to be the same way.

19. Don't take it personal!

Whatever your baby daddy does or does not do, don't take it personal. Most of the times, his actions are not even about you. It's just the way he was raised or a result of his beliefs, thinking, attitude or bad decisions. Let him be him and you focus on just being who God has designed you to be. Remember only God has the power to transform lives and you can't change him. If you don't like his ways, don't take it personal, just pray for him and let God create a change! There is a purpose for your pain and that purpose is to make you better. Keep your eyes on God and keep moving forward.

20. Train up your child God's way!

The Bible teaches us to train up a child in the way he should go and when he is old he will not depart from it (Proverb 22:6). It is so important for baby mama's to train their kids up in the right ways according to the Word of God. There are so many negative influences, traps and temptations in this world that we must be sure to equip our children with everything they need to live successful lives on earth as well as have access to everlasting life with Jesus in Heaven. The world we live in today will eat our children alive, if we don't prepare them and train them up properly. This world is quick to make a statistic out of our children because of our baby mama status. Baby mama's can and do raise successful, emotionally stable, productive kids who are contributing members of the society. There are no barriers to kids who have the Lord on their side, so train them up right! The seeds of greatness we plant in our children today will determine the harvest we receive in them tomorrow.

21. Discipline your kids because you love them!

Don't let the devil or anybody else make you feel bad about disciplining your kids. It's your job as a parent to discipline them and if you don't do it now, later the police and the correction officers will. Discipline your child because you love them but be careful not to let discipline drift into child abuse. Always strive to discipline out of love and not anger. Proverbs 22:15 say foolishness is bound in the heart of a child, but the rod of correction shall drive it far from him. God disciplines us because He loves us and wants to keep us from hell so if we love our kids and want to keep them from hell, we will do the same thing (Proverbs 23:13-14, 19:18 & 13:24). You know your child or children and God does too, so pray to God that He gives you a disciplinary system that works best for you and your kids. If you refuse to discipline your children while they are young, one day they may be disciplining you.

22. Take your kids to church & keep them active in extracurricular activities!

By taking your kids to church (not just any church but the church that God has lead you to and placed you and your family in) you help them further develop their relationship with God and other believers (Hebrews10: 25). You teach them how to praise and worship God, order, discipline, how to hear from God and how to receive His word. Keep your kids active in church, so that they can learn early that they were born to serve God and His people. By keeping your kids active in church activities and other beneficial extracurricular activities, you will teach them responsibility and keep them from being idle and open to the foolishness of the devil and this world.

23. Take trips with your kids!

Even if your budget doesn't permit you going to Disney World or Paris, take your kids on a family trip every year. Good memories can be made anywhere and learning takes place wherever we go. A good family trip doesn't have to cost a fortune. Be creative, be strategic and plan ahead to create good memorable experiences for you and your kids. In learning, experience matters, it determines your kids knowledgebase and vocabulary. Visit museums, national parks, parks, go to plays, go the movies, site see, etc. Be consistent about providing your child with opportunities to explore the earth, go places, experience new things and meet new people. Don't limit your kids to spending their entire lives never leaving their neighborhood.

24. Be apart of a good network of parents!

There are some great people that God has placed in your life to help you with your kids. Don't take advantage of them but appreciate them. These people are a blessing and an asset to you and your children. If you don't have this type of network, pray for it because as a single mother, it helps to have some help with your kids. Be careful not to be the baby mama who always sends her child with somebody else. Be open to help other mothers with their kids as well. This may be an old saying but today it is still very true, it takes a village to successfully raise kids.

25. Don't trust everybody with your kids!

When allowing people to help you with your kids, you must be very careful. Some adults and even children are perpetrators and predators looking to prey on your kids. Always pray over your children and with your children before you send them out in the world. Use discernment and wisdom when allowing your child to go with another family or person. Also keep the lines of communication open with your child so that they will feel comfortable talking to you about everything. That way if something foul has taken place, your kid will be in the best position to let you know. As a baby mama, you are venerable to predators because they know you need the help and they will offer what seems like innocent assistance to you just so they can get close to your kids. Be careful, your kids can't go with everybody and everybody cannot be around your kids.

26. Quiet time, you need it!

Start off everyday with some quiet time, with just you and the Lord. Even Jesus started His day off with quiet time (Mark 1:35). Get up early before the kids, read your Bible, listen to God, collect your thoughts and pray. You will be amazed how much smoother your day will be when you start your morning off with this quiet time with God. Psalms 5:3 says, "My voice shalt thou hear in the morning, O Lord: in the morning will I direct my prayer unto thee and will look up." Let God be the first one you talk with everyday. With the demands that being a baby mama can bring, you may think that you don't have time for quiet time. The truth is, you won't have peace without it. Pray to God for strength to help you steal some quiet time each and every day. This time alone with God will transform your life and empower you to keep going strong. This time will equip you with what you need to be a successfully Christian, mother, worker and friend.

27. Don't forget your "me" time!

You love your kids but you; yes you need some time alone away from them. Take yourself out on a date, read a book, watch a movie, go on a mini vacation, etc. Every so often take some time to be on your own. Learn how to love and enjoy yourself because that will keep you in the position to love and enjoy your kids. There is nothing wrong with having some fun without the kids. Let your hair down, smile and let the fun begin.

28. Treat yourself!

Don't forget to treat yourself. You deserve it after all the work that you do to keep your home running effectively. Don't allow anyone to make you feel bad about spending money on yourself. Put yourself in the budget every month or every other month (based on what you can afford of course). Buy a new dress, get your hair done, get your nails done, and buy yourself some ice cream, lunch or dinner. Don't wait for somebody else to recognize you and treat you, step up and treat yourself!

29. Avoid becoming anybody else's baby mama!

Hey you already have a baby daddy or two. Don't add another one to your list. The more baby daddies you have to deal with, the more complicated your life will become. Having all these kids with all these different men not only negatively affects you but it also negatively affects your kids. Sex outside of marriage really does complicate things that God designed to be simple. As a baby mama you are already know the price you've had to pay for your previous disobedience. Don't make your life or the lives of your kids harder than they have to be. Pray to God that He will send you the husband he created just for you and your family. God even said himself that it's not good for man to be alone (Genesis2: 18-25). You are some man's rib, so pray to God that your husband finds you soon. Be ready when he comes and save the sex for the honeymoon because that will be the man God designed just for you and your kids.

30. Stop the cycle!

If your mama was a baby mama, your grand mama was a baby mama, your great grand mama was a baby mama and you're a baby mama, your family is in a generational curse. A generational curse is a bad habit or negative stronghold that is passed down through generations of your family. It's passed down in the spiritual realm. It may or may not be intentional but your wondering how does this keep happening. How do the woman in my family keep falling into the same thing and how do I keep this from happening to my daughter. After all that you've been through on your baby mama journey, I know that you do not want this same fate for your kids. Since you're the one reading this book, its up to you to break the cycle and end the baby mama generational curse.

1. If you are saved, great! But if you are not saved, you must be! Ask Jesus Christ to come into your heart and save you today. He is faithful and He will save you, just acknowledge him and ask.
2. Stop fornicating and shacking. If he is your God ordained husband, he will care about your soul and the souls of your children.
3. When you make a mistake don't give up, get up ask for forgiveness and get back on the right track again.
4. Keep it real and be transparent with yourself and God.
5. Ask God for help with every part of the process.
6. Have self-control. Don't be afraid to tell yourself no.
7. Fast and pray. Pray for your self, your kids and their daddy.
8. Read, read and reread. Read the Bible and other books about soul ties and generational curses. You will be amazed what you discover.
9. Keep the lines of communication open with your kids at all times, ages and stages of their lives. Talk to your kids and be open with them about your flaws and the consequences you have had to face as a result of your decisions.
10. Share what you know and have learned through the years because people perish for a lack of knowledge.

11. Love and nurture your kids so that they will not go looking for love in all the wrong places.
12. Lay a solid foundation with your kids based on God's Word.
13. Teach your daughter the importance and the severity of her remaining pure until marriage.
14. Be a resource to your kids, challenge them and encourage them to do more and make better decisions than you did.
15. There is power in the Jesus, consistently plead the blood of Jesus over you and your kids.
16. Speak the blessing and speak life over your children and grand children. Show them, who they are to Jesus, show them their worth to Him, what He paid for them and how much they mean to Him. Teach them how to make positive declarations over themselves.

Chapter Ten

How to Avoid Becoming a Baby Mama

Premarital Sex/ Extramarital Sex…..Just don't do it!!!

Having sex with him before marriage is not going to give you the results you want!

Chapter Eleven

Meet the Real Baby Mamas

Latisha is the mother of two children, Nia Elise and Kenley. She is a baby mama and has been a baby mama for the past 11 years. Her mother was a baby mama, her grand mother was a baby mama and her great grandmother was a baby mama. Her experiences being a baby mama and being a child of a baby mama led to the writing of this book. Latisha has been writing since the age of 13 and has used writing as a tool to express herself. Since becoming a baby mama, Latisha has gone on to live a very successful and productive life. The birth of her daughter in 2004 led to her getting serious about college and completing her first degree. The birth of her son in 2009, led to her accepting JESUS CHRIST as her LORD and Savior. Her children have been a major blessing in her life and the lives of others. Being saved and converted is her greatest accomplishment. While being a baby mama, she has obtained a Bachelor's of Science degree, a Master's degree, National Board Teaching certification and is currently pursing a PhD. Latisha is the co-founder of I.D.E.A.L. Women at the

University of Southern Mississippi. She has been the guest speaker at several induction ceremonies and other events. Latisha is known for sharing empowering motivational messages. She shares the WORD of GOD every Monday on the Morning Glory call, which reaches people throughout the United States. Her Facebook page, DivineHealing Touch provides encouragement to over 2,600 people. Latisha is an active member of her church (Mt. Carmel Ministries) and of the community. Latisha has a passion for sharing her love of CHRIST and encouraging and motivating others. For years, Latisha struggled emotionally being a baby mama but through her relationship with God, she has become an overcomer. In July of 2015, Latisha married her best friend, James Pitts.

Sharon is from Cleveland, Ohio and now resides in Murrieta, California. Sharon relocated to California in 2013 from Forth Worth, Texas. She is currently married and has 3 younger children at home and 3 adult children, one living in Georgia, one living in Mississippi (Latisha) and one living in Texas (Tekeirra). Sharon started writing at the age of 11 and wrote her first play titled, "Love, Hate, Marriage and Divorce" when she was 11 years old. It took her one-year to complete the play. She continued to write throughout the years and wrote several song lyrics, greeting card greetings, short stories and a poetry book with over 100 different poems. She founded and was in the all-girl singing group, "Versatile" in 1997, however the group ended up breaking up a year later. Sharon continued to pursue her dreams of being in the entertainment field by continue to write and manage her daughters' singing and dancing careers. Throughout all of her struggles of being a baby mama at the age of 17, and dealing with personal problems arising from being a baby mama, she has strived throughout her life to take care of her family in the most beneficial and loving manner. Sharon believes that baby mamas must be courageous and continue to go forward in life no matter how difficult the journey is, knowing that the Lord is with them throughout the every step of the way. Believing in herself, having faith and being courageous have aided Sharon in the successful completion of her Associate of Applied Science degree in Business Management and the successful completion of her Bachelors of Science degree in Management. As a married baby mama Sharon understands the struggles, heartaches and problems that some baby mama's face and that is why she felt the need to contribute to this book. She believes in being dedicated to whatever your dreams are and doing what is necessary to make them come true. In the beginning Sharon was a baby mama, who accomplished many things and know that you too can do the same as long as you're willing to go for it.

Tekeirra was born on June 17th, 1994 in Decatur, Ga. The youngest child of three children, she was considered the baby at that time. She was a happy baby and her mother always referred to her as 'bookie bear". As Tekeirra grew up, around the age of 14, she started to want to be in plays, sing and dance. She was in acting competitions at her school and singing and modeling contest around Atlanta. Around 2008 her family relocated to Texas. Of course, she wasn't happy about the move and didn't want to do go, but it wasn't up to her. Tekeirra went to live with her sister (Latisha) for the summer and while there, her older sister taught her how to have self respect, how to act, and how to treat others. Her older sister is a big influence on her life along with her mother, and they have both really helped her change her life around. While in Texas, Tekeirra started to grow up and talk to guys, and ended up meeting one that would end up changing her life forever. Tekeirra became a baby mama at the young age of eighteen. While visiting her sister, she accepted Jesus Christ as her Lord and Savior. While pregnant, she rededicated her life to Christ and got baptized on July 7th, 2012. Tekeirra is currently a full time mother of two and a college student. Since becoming a baby mama, she has been a guest speaker at several teen pregnancy prevention events. She currently maintains a YouTube page called, Kierraandbaby, where she encourages and offers support to other teen moms. Her YouTube page has over 1,200 subscribers with over 9, 000 video views. Tekeirra is a baby mama and she is an inspiration to many.

The King James Bible is used as a reference throughout this book.

www.ingramcontent.com/pod-product-compliance
Lightning Source LLC
Chambersburg PA
CBHW072022060426
42449CB00034B/1658